THE TROUBLE WITH CULTURE

THE TROUBLE
WITH CULTURE

---

*How Computers
are Calming
the Culture Wars*

F. Allan Hanson

STATE UNIVERSITY OF NEW YORK PRESS

Published by
State University of New York Press, Albany

For information, address State University of New York Press,
194 Washington Avenue, Suite 305, Albany, NY 12210-2384

Production by Michael Haggett
Marketing by Michael Campochiaro

Library of Congress Cataloging in Publication Data

Hanson, F. Allan, 1939–
 The trouble with culture : how computers are calming the culture wars / F. Allan Hanson.
   p. cm.
 Includes bibliographical references (p.   ) and index.
 ISBN-13: 978-0-7914-7017-6 (hardcover : alk. paper)
 ISBN-13: 978-0-7914-7018-3 (pbk. : alk. paper) 1. Information technology—Social
aspects. 2. Culture. 3. Classification—Social aspects. 4. Indexing—Social aspects.
I. Title

HM851.H35 2007
303.48'33—dc22

2006020753

10 9 8 7 6 5 4 3 2 1

For Daniel, Kennedy, Jack, Owen, and Adam

Contents

Acknowledgments

―――――――――――――――――

This book owes its existence to the generous support of numerous institutions and individuals. I am grateful for a research grant (0092618) from the National Science Foundation, a senior fellowship from the National Endowment for the Humanities, a faculty fellowship from the University of Kansas Hall Center for the Humanities, and a summer grant from the University of Kansas General Research Fund. Warm thanks also go to research assistants Shawna Carroll, Quincy McCrary, Heather Meiers, and Mark Stahl. Shawna and Quincy contributed to the project in multiple ways, while Heather and Mark undertook more focused tasks. Much of my research took the form of interviews with individuals from both coasts and the midwest. I spoke to federal and state judges, practicing attorneys, and faculty members in the fields of law, English and journalism. They are too numerous to mention by name, but I am deeply grateful to all of them for their patience, interest, and willingness to help. As in all things, my wife, Louise Hanson, was a rich source of ideas, criticism, and encouragement from start to finish.

Chapter 1

Culture Gone Bad

Culture has turned sour. Originally a constructive force, it has now become disruptive to contemporary society. A seldom-recognized factor in the troubled relation between culture and society is automated information technology, the most influential technological development of our time. Automation's role is ambivalent. In some ways it is used to increase culture's disruptive influence, but the main line of my argument will be that in more subtle but important ways it acts to lessen it. The primary objectives of this book are to explain how and why culture has gone bad and to explore what automated information technology has to do with it.

CULTURE

One of the most poetic descriptions of culture, used by Ruth Benedict in her famous book *Patterns of Culture*, comes from a Digger Indian of California: "In the beginning God gave to every people a cup, a cup of clay, and from this cup they drank their life. . . . Our cup is broken now. It has passed away" (Benedict 1934:21–22). The metaphor of culture as a cup from which people drink their lives captures the pervasiveness of culture in all things human. Culture consists of language and the systems of meanings and symbols—beliefs regarding the natural and supernatural world, moral imperatives, customs of all sorts—that have furnished the rich variety of human designs for living. Strictly speaking, culture may not be an exclusively human possession, for dolphins and whales have audible systems of communication, chimpanzees and pet dogs learn patterns of acting that could be called customs, and many other aspects of animal behavior are claimed to qualify in one way or another as cultural. But it is still fair to say that culture has set us apart from other species, because none of them comes anywhere close to the complexity and variety of human cultures.

Indeed, more than setting humans apart from other species, one can even say that culture has made our species what it is. That is, prior to becoming *Homo sapiens,* our hominid ancestors possessed certain trappings of culture, such as the ability to use fire and to make tools. Therefore, culture was one of the environmental conditions to which certain aspects of our biological makeup—certainly our brains, and perhaps our hands and other characteristics—adapted in the latter stages of human evolution. We are, that is to say, biologically formed to have culture (Washburn 1959; Muller 1959:2–3; Geertz 1973a, 1973b; D'Andrade 2002). Not any particular culture, because its particulars are learned and not transmitted genetically, but without culture of some sort we would not be fully human.

If anthropologists and others have manifested any concern about the overall status of culture, then it is the danger of certain cultures being emasculated or taken away.[1] This is an outcome of rapid social change, as in the circumstances of conquest and colonialism. The loss of land and means of livelihood due to large-scale settlement by foreigners has been especially lethal to indigenous cultures. The plight of Native Americans and Australian aborigines, who have been displaced by populations with a radically different technology and way of life, is poignantly articulated by the Digger Indian quoted above and is all too familiar to everyone.

While I have no wish to dispute or minimize such tragic injustices, this book builds on the different premise that if there is a general problem with culture in the contemporary world, then it is not that there is too little of it but, quite to the contrary, too much. In the pages that follow I will argue that culture is now working at cross-purposes with society. Culture and society are different things, and they have followed different courses of evolution. A society is a human group, an organized plurality of interacting individuals, while culture, as I have said, refers to beliefs, meanings, symbols, and customs that are shared by members of human groups. In the early phases of human existence, society and culture worked well together, when culture was an important force for maintaining and integrating society. In the course of evolution, society has changed dramatically from small, simple, face-to-face bands to large, internally diverse nation states. Culture, for its part, has changed in response to the growth of society, but in such a way that it now plays a divisive role in today's large, complex societies.

The other primary objective of this book is to contend that recent technological developments in the automation of information are highly pertinent to this situation. They are pertinent to it, however, in an ambivalent manner. The greater part of my discussion aims to demonstrate how they act to alleviate the discord between culture and society. Yet it will also be necessary to recognize how, in other ways, they exacerbate the discord. But before getting into that, we need to look more closely at the relation between society and culture and their divergent evolutionary paths.

SOCIAL AND CULTURAL EVOLUTION

Culture emerged as an adaptive strategy in the conditions of prehuman and early human social life. These consisted of small, more or less nomadic groups that gained their livelihood from wild plants and animals and engaged in friendly or hostile interactions with other, similar groups. They developed ideas that defined their relation to the natural and supernatural world, articulated norms regarding proper and improper behavior, and entertained themselves with games, jokes, and stories. Common language, beliefs, values, and expectations enabled members of such groups to live and work together effectively and to distinguish themselves from other groups, with other cultures. Archaeologists trace the growing importance and complexity of shared understandings and learned behavior in residue left in pigment and stone and bone. The earliest tools testify to the realization that the environment could be exploited more effectively by modifying certain natural products. Later refinements of that idea are visible in more advanced tools tailored to specialized activities such as piercing, cutting, and scraping. Early art in the form of paintings and sculptures of animal and human figures reveals the development of aesthetic senses of form, proportion, and color. Venus figures of heavy-breasted, pregnant women may express ideas about human fertility, while sculptures and paintings of animals and hunting scenes may depict beliefs regarding the relation between hunters and their quarry. Mortuary customs such as burial, placing bodies in certain postures, coloring the bones, and depositing various objects with them all reveal that human groups were beginning to conceptualize death as an existential issue and were developing ideas about its relation to life and an afterlife. Although it left no material remains, the development of language was an essential aspect of the early growth of culture.

Ethnographic accounts of hunting-and-gathering peoples from Australia, Africa, and the Americas have greatly enriched our understanding of small-scale societies. Book after book describes the marvelous variety of their social and political organizations, their religious and magical beliefs, their knowledge of plants, animals, and the natural world, their ideas about illness and healing, and their folklore and mythology. Although human beings have never been robotic slaves to custom, incapable of independent thought, culture does stress common beliefs and conventions. These enabled people of simple societies to communicate with each other through language and other systems of symbols and to coordinate their economic, social, political, ideological, and recreational activities to conduct the necessary tasks of daily life, maximize their chances for survival, and hold a set of understandings and values to give life meaning, purpose, and beauty.

Sharing the same language, understandings, and values does more than just enable individuals to communicate and interact easily with each other. In small, relatively simple, societies culture is the basis of social solidarity, the glue that holds society together. People identify themselves as Arunta or Cheyenne or Mbuti because a common culture—language, beliefs, values, customs—ties them to each other and simultaneously distinguishes them from other groups with other cultures. In his classic *The Division of Labor in Society*, Emile Durkheim (1933) called this form of social cohesion "mechanical solidarity."

It is important to recognize that culture works best to provide mechanical solidarity when it is closed: when its tenets are clear, unequivocal, and fixed, and when its adherents accept them as unquestionably true, support them ardently, and reject alternatives out of hand. Dissent, or even lukewarm acquiescence, weakens the consensus. Thus Durkheim argued that mechanical solidarity demands strict conformity with the common sentiments, beliefs, values, and customs. Any breach or flaunting of them constitutes a serious threat to social stability. Hence, the law that upholds them tends to be repressive, even vengeful. Harsh punishments preserve social cohesiveness by reinforcing the centrality and rightness of the common culture (Durkheim 1933:80–88, 102–103).

Closed culture is most successful when the scale is small and relatively isolated. A consensus of beliefs and expectations is easiest to maintain when held by restricted numbers of people who are in regular contact with each other. Conflicts that might emerge from encounters between different cultures pose a relatively low risk when people do not have much to do with outsiders.

But small, self-sufficient, and isolated societies are now rare. The vast majority of human beings today belong to large, complex societies that have tens or hundreds of millions of members and encompass diverse subcultures. The initial cause of the shift was the Neolithic or Agricultural Revolution, which refers to the time about 10,000 years ago when people first domesticated plants. This dramatically increased the capacity to produce food. People abandoned nomadic wandering for sedentary residences, the population increased, and towns and cities came into being. Increases in the variety and prevalence of material possessions and in population density led certain people to specialize as craftsmen, traders, soldiers, priests, and administrators. Thus the division of labor, which with hunting-and-gathering technology is largely limited to sex and age, became much more elaborate.

Several nineteenth-century scholars noted that the basis of social solidarity changed as societies became larger and more diverse. Instead of the cultural similarity that constitutes mechanical solidarity, societies with a complex division of labor are held together by their *differences:* the cobbler depends on the baker for bread, who depends on the carpenter for shelter, who depends on the blacksmith for tools, who depends on the cobbler for shoes. With this kind of economic interdependence, it did not matter so much that people thought and believed the same things and looked at the world in a distinctive way. Therefore, common culture became less important, and individual variability increased. On the analogy with the different, interdependent physiological functions of the organs of the body, Durkheim (1933) named this kind of social cohesiveness "organic solidarity" (p. 131).

Durkheim insisted, however, that organic solidarity entails more than just economic interdependence. It ushers in changes in law, religion, and morality, and it liberates the individual. This contrasts sharply with mechanical solidarity, which "is strong only if the individual is not. . . . [I]t receives from . . . universal, uniform practice an authority which bestows something superhuman upon it, and which puts it beyond the pale of discussion. The co-operative society [with organic solidarity], on the contrary, develops in the measure that individual personality becomes stronger" (p. 228). Under organic solidarity, for example, law becomes concerned more with restoring the aggrieved individual to the state that obtained before an offense than to uphold the tenets of common culture (p. 111). Religious belief, all-pervasive under mechanical solidarity, goes into retreat (p. 169). This is "linked to the fundamental conditions of the development of societies, and it shows that there is a decreasing number of collective beliefs and sentiments which are both collective enough and strong enough to take on a religious character. That is to say, the average intensity of the common conscience progressively becomes enfeebled" (p. 170).

Even something as apparently inconsequential as the declining use of proverbs reveals the same trend. Noting that "a proverb is a condensed statement of a collective idea or sentiment relative to a determined category of objects," Durkheim (1933) writes that "the decrease in the number of proverbs, adages, dicta, etc. as societies develop, is another proof that the collective representations move towards indetermination" (p. 170). In other words, just as differences between human individuals become more pronounced, so do differences between conceptualizations of situations and events. This makes it more difficult to classify them in a few preestablished categories. Therefore, the use of proverbs and adages, which serve to lump situations and events in precisely such categories, becomes less apt.

As these passages make clear, Durkheim (1933) understood the development of the more complex division of labor and the associated transition from mechanical to organic solidarity in terms of evolution to a more advanced state of both the individual and society (see also pp. 129–31, 152). Although more stress is placed on unity of thought in mechanical solidarity, it does not follow that society becomes less cohesive with the ascent of organic solidarity. In fact, for Durkheim (1933), organic solidarity is the stronger glue. "Social progress . . . does not consist in a continual dissolution. On the contrary, the more we advance, the more profoundly do societies reveal the sentiment of self and of unity . . . even where it is most resistant, mechanical solidarity does not link men with the same force as the division of labor" (p. 173, see also p. 151). Nor did Durkheim (1933) think that the cultural sentiments and understandings that underpin mechanical solidarity are in danger of vanishing all together. "This is not to say . . . that the common conscience is threatened with total disappearance. Only, it more and more comes to consist of very general and very indeterminate ways of thinking and feeling, which leave an open place for a growing multitude of individual differences" (p. 172). Culture, that is, becomes more open because people become more open-minded. Culture's tenets lose their absolute and imperative qualities. Individuals develop freedom of thought to the point that they can regard the principles of their culture dispassionately, even critically, and can consider the merits of alternatives to them.

OPEN AND CLOSED CULTURE

Durkheim recognized that the division of labor did not, alas, invariably produce greater social cohesion and the advances toward equality of opportunity, individual expression, and the other trappings of open culture that ideally characterize organic solidarity. These beneficial outcomes occur when differences are recognized as complementary, enhancing each other. But two other kinds of difference may also result from the division of labor, both of them deleterious. One is contradiction (Durkheim 1933:55–56). Here different constituencies are set against each other in a zero-sum game where any gain of one is thought to come at the expense of another. The vast inequities of wealth and power in an industrial system, for example, give rise to frustrations and antagonisms as the rich exploit the poor (pp. 354–56). Another example of contradiction is a caste system that allocates positions of privilege or inferiority according to birth, thus denying equal opportunity on the basis of the natural distribution of talents (pp. 380–81). The second kind of deleterious difference, which I call compartmental, occurs when the division of labor generates distinct elements that function in isolation from each other. In this event, the mutual benefits of coordination are not realized. Durkheim's (1933) main example is the blinkered development of the various scientific disciplines, each oblivious to what is happening in the others and ignorant of the progress that would result from bringing their different perspectives to bear on common problems (pp. 356–57).

According to Durkheim, the more culture is closed, the more it limits the latitude and expression of individual judgment. That is released to develop when culture opens to the point that people are not imprisoned by its tenets but can regard them dispassionately and rationally consider alternatives. But they can consider alternatives only when they know that there *are* alternatives, and that occurs primarily in the conditions of regular contact between different societies and within large, culturally heterogeneous societies. Even then, however, individual judgment flourishes only when cultural differences are deemed complementary, with the potential to mesh effectively. Large societies with a complex division of labor but with contradictory or compartmental differences among their constituent cultures retain the same cultural closure and correspondingly restricted individuality characteristic of small, homogeneous societies with mechanical solidarity. Compulsive adherence to one set of ideas and values while condemning all alternatives as dangerous or evil is the stuff, as we shall see in the next chapter, of culture wars and other cultural conflicts. And to compartmentalize differences is to encourage people to cocoon themselves complacently in the received views of their own culture, avoiding the challenge or threat that comes with taking other views seriously.

Durkheim (1933) held that the natural result of the division of labor is what we have called open culture: the perception of differences as complementary and all the benefits that flow from the attendant organic solidarity. What we have called contradictory and compartmental differences, with their detrimental consequences, are in his eyes exceptional and abnormal results of the division of labor (pp. 353–54, 372). He distinguished three abnormal or pathological forms, two of which are of interest here. One of these, the anomic division of labor, occurs when different parts of the system do not interact smoothly together, either because proper communications between them are somehow obstructed or have not had sufficient time to become established (pp. 368–69). The meaninglessness of work for assembly-line workers comes about because there has not been enough time to adjust to the new conditions of industrialization. Nor has there been adequate time for the different branches of science to accommodate each other, the problem being especially acute in the social sciences because they are the youngest ones. But Durkheim (1933) was confident that with time these imperfections would work themselves out (pp. 370–71).

He refers to another abnormal form as the forced division of labor (pp. 374–88). This occurs, as it does all too frequently, when rewards and opportunities are allocated on the basis of heredity or cronyism instead of according to the natural distribution of talents. This occurs when power is distributed unevenly in society and those with it use it to exploit and hold down those without it. The forced division of labor spawns many of the evils that complex societies are heir to: poverty, injustice, resentment, and, in the effort to undo them, revolution. Durkheim (1933) fully acknowledges that these evils (his word, p. 387) persist, but he insists that their days are numbered. Justice and equality are systemically braided into organic solidarity, and the progress of the division of labor necessitates their realization. "No matter how important the progress already realized in this direction, it gives, in all likelihood, only a small idea of what will be realized in the future" (p. 381).

Durkheim's view that the anomic and forced forms of the division of labor are pathological, in the sense that they are harmful, may well be accepted today, but I do not think that they would be viewed as abnormal. In 1893, when *The Division of Labor* was originally published, Durkheim was clearly a believer in progress. Along with most of his contemporaries, he was convinced that society is advancing to a higher state of freedom, equality, individuality, and justice. Too, one gets the impression that he became somewhat carried away with the perfectly interdependent organs in a biological organism (specifically, a mammal) as a metaphor for human society with organic solidarity. Today we are more prone to believe that power and domination are constantly endemic to human affairs, and we are less likely to think of society as being or becoming so well integrated (as, indeed, our increasing understanding of the immune system and disorders such as HIV make biological organisms appear less seamlessly organized).

While Durkheim would see what we have called complementary difference as natural and explain complementary and compartmental differences in terms of his abnormal forms, my opinion is that the development of large societies with a complex division of labor is more likely to generate contradictory and compartmental differences than complementary ones. Part of the reason for this is that I, along with most of my contemporaries, do not share Durkheim's general faith in progress. The other part has to do with culture. Unlike Durkheim, I think culture itself—what he calls the collective consciousness, and what he sees as the basis of mechanical solidarity—is a contributing factor to contradictory and compartmental difference. Cultural difference is an important reason communication between parts of complex societies becomes occluded and powerful constituencies are all too ready to exercise domination and exclusion (and weak constituencies to resent and rebel). This is what I call the trouble with culture.

The source of the trouble lurks along the intertwined evolutionary paths of society and culture. Closed culture is an entirely workable adaptation to societies that are simple, small, and relatively isolated. A primary function of culture in such circumstances is to provide the mechanical solidarity that holds such societies together, and this works best when culture is inward looking. That is, it acts primarily to order the relations among people within the society. As society evolved to become large and internally complex, it increasingly incorporated a number of different cultures defined along any of a variety of lines, such as ethnicity, class, wealth, religion, gender, sexual preference, and so on. In response to that, culture evolved to become outward looking. At least as much as regulating relations among its adherents, culture now serves as a mark of identity that people from different constituencies use to define themselves in terms of the distinctive characteristics that set them apart from each other. This is benignly visible in innumerable street fairs and community festivals and more ominously so in ethnic and religious clashes around the world.

As it turns outward, culture may open or it may remain closed. The proximity and regular encounter of cultural differences in complex, heterogeneous societies might loosen the grip of culture on its adherents, encouraging them to recognize and appreciate ways of thinking and behaving different from their own. In that case, the loosening of cultural imperatives and expansion of individual thought and freedom signal an opening of culture to the harmonious coexistence of complementary differences that Durkheim associated with organic solidarity. But more commonly, as some societies, or groups within or between societies, corner power and dominate others, culture maintains or even increases its closed quality as it becomes enlisted as a political weapon in the struggle between groups bent on maintaining or overthrowing various forms of hegemony (Turner 1993:423–24). Narrow-mindedness and intolerance or indifference toward other values and understandings are rampant as hostile attitudes and behavior fly between societies in regular contact, as well as between culturally different constituencies within the same society. This is the trouble with culture. It has become a divisive factor in the contemporary conditions of globalization and large, internally diverse societies.

Examples are everywhere. Specialized constituencies develop their own interests and points of view. Bureaucrats have different needs and see things differently than the intelligentsia, who differ in these ways from the military, who differ again from farmers or industrial workers. They develop different cultures. Moreover, empires and nation-states formed societies that encompass several different ethnic and cultural groups. They too see things differently. If the differences are such that people feel threatened by them, then they come into more or less open conflict and are therefore the type of difference we have called contradictory. If they are perceived as irrelevant, or if cultural differences are used as a tool for excluding people from certain groups or positions in society, then they coexist in isolation from each other and are compartmental. Both of these outcomes demonstrate that culture, originally well adapted to the small, homogeneous communities that characterized the early conditions of human life, has become maladapted to the heterogeneous societies in which most human beings live today.

In viewing cultural difference within contemporary societies as maladapted, I seem to be bucking a current in contemporary thought that celebrates cultural diversity. Too often, however, that stream is shallow. When my family visited Disneyland some years ago, we piled into small boats and were ferried through a series of artificial landscapes ranging from Alpine pastures to Asian rice paddies to central African villages. Animated dolls peopled each location, of a color and in costumes ethnically appropriate to it, all smiling and swaying and singing "It's a small world, after all." The experience was annoying, partly because I could not get the tune out of my head and partly because it trivialized cultural differences. Of course we enjoy the cultural diversity of costume and cuisine, folklore, and music and dance in restaurants and concert halls and at street fairs and community festivals. But culture more fundamentally concerns convictions about the texture of reality, the shape of the divine, the nature of truth, and the morality of behavior. In the environment of closed culture, when differences of these sorts butt up against each other, what they evoke ranges from shouting matches between talking heads on television to street demonstrations to terrorist attacks and war. As societies interact more frequently and become internally more diverse, such dangerous and divisive confrontations increase. That, again, is the trouble with culture. What is needed is not more polka bands and street dances (although I certainly do not recommend less of them, because they are a lot of fun and probably do make some modest contribution toward solving the problem) but to cool down and open up cultural principles to the point where they lose their absolute, imperative trappings and can be weighed, considered, and appreciated by open-minded individuals as representatives of a multitude of designs for human living.

To summarize, the evolutionary paths of culture and society have diverged to the point where culture has become an obstacle to the productive communication and interaction that it originally enabled. For it again to become a positive aspect of social life, people must free themselves from being so exclusively and irrevocably saturated with their own cultural premises that they are existentially threatened by alternatives. This does not mean, as Durkheim pointed out, that culture would disappear altogether. That is virtually unthinkable, because then the languages and shared concepts that are necessary for communication and interaction would be lacking. What it does mean is that culture must open to the point that people can gain critical understanding of and control over their cultural principles and concepts rather than being held in thrall to them. This is much deeper than a Disneyland celebration of cultural diversity. It requires building bridges between the most basic of cultural premises and juxtaposing cultural differences in a rational way that encourages the formation of new ideas and strategies. This can occur only in the circumstances of open culture that make it possible to see those differences as complementary rather than contradictory or compartmental.

AUTOMATION: A PREVIEW

The automation of information or the "computer revolution" has important consequences for the evolution of culture that cut in both directions. On the one hand, it enables certain cultures to become even more closed as mass communication and computer-mediated communication promote "narrowcasting." People now can immerse themselves in television channels and Internet communities that reinforce their preconceived ways of thinking and never mention alternatives except to denigrate them.

The primary emphasis of this book, however, is on the other side: the less recognized, more subtle, but pervasive ways that automated techniques for storing, accessing, and using information foster evolution toward a more open culture. Briefly, to prefigure the argument that will fill many of the following pages, in the nonautomated context, events and ideas are categorized according to fixed classification schemes ordained by culture. This reinforces received ways of thinking and is therefore conducive to contradictory and compartmental differences. In contrast, automated information management techniques such as keyword searching are fluid and contingent, expressly tailored to specific circumstances such as the particular terms of a search query. This often juxtaposes bits of information in novel ways, challenging the user to develop creative interpretations.

Automation opens culture by loosening its certainties. Thought is less constrained by prefabricated categories, and judgments become more flexible. Cultural differences appear less as contradictory and threatening and more as complementary and with interesting possibilities for common ground. This change of mind-set stimulates evolution toward a more open culture, with the potential to calm the culture wars and bring culture into a more harmonious, productive relation with today's large-scale, heterogeneous societies.

AN OVERVIEW

The next chapter takes a more thorough look at the trouble with culture, including how automated information technology may exacerbate it, bolstered by examples of how culture has disrupted contemporary and historical societies by fostering contradictory and compartmental differences within and between them. But forces are also abroad that work to open culture, thus encouraging the recognition of complementary differences and assisting the spread of organic solidarity. Chapter 3 addresses three such forces. Two of them—cultural relativism and postmodernism—have been relatively ineffective. The third, which shows considerably more promise, is the automation of information. The remainder of the book explores those little recognized social consequences of automation that counteract culture's divisiveness and promote organic solidarity.

Human intelligence and artificial intelligence organize and access information differently. Human intelligence stresses classifying, while artificial intelligence relies more on indexing. This apparently drab distinction spawns enough important consequences that several chapters will be required to plumb it adequately. Chapter 4 discusses the central importance of classifying to culture, and chapter 5 fleshes out that discussion with a case study of the role and far-reaching implications of classifying in the common law. Chapter 6 introduces the concept of indexing and explains its affinity for automation. Chapters 7 and 8 explore the various consequences of indexing for opening culture and promoting organic solidarity, with the help of several case studies drawn from recent developments in the law as well as education, scholarly research, and business and manufacturing practices.

Chapter 9 explores a different but related set of consequences of automation, arguing that among the many developments it supports is a far-reaching change in our concept of ourselves as persons, individuals, or agents. Closed culture thrives on fixed, definite, unquestioned categories, and one of the most invariable categories of all is the notion of the determinate human individual. But today the increasing participation of artificial intelligence in the conduct of many activities renders the methodological individualist strategy of explaining social action entirely in terms of human individuals as untenable. The chapter develops a "superorganic" concept of agency, consisting of variable combinations of human, mechanical, electronic, and other components that form specifically to undertake particular actions and reform in other configurations for other actions. The contingent, recombinant quality of superorganic agency undermines the unequivocal, fixed assumptions that mark closed culture and paves the way toward the flexibility characteristic of open culture.

Chapter 10 concludes the work by drawing the main points together and advancing the basic argument that automation is an antidote for the trouble with culture. It weakens cultural absolutism by encouraging independent and creative thinking. This mind-set, characteristic of open culture, is tuned to recognize cultural differences as being complementary rather than automatically condemning them as erroneous or irrelevant. This can cool the culture wars and help align the evolution of culture with that of society.

When I embarked upon this project, a friend warned, "Be careful. That's a moving target." A topic that is developing as rapidly as information technology carries, on the one hand, the danger that much of what one writes may be obsolete by the time it reaches print and, on the other hand, the temptation to engage in speculation. Imagining an indeterminably distant future, for example, some visionaries have predicted that just as eons ago biological organisms freed themselves from the limitations of the inorganic matter from which they emerged, so artificial intelligence may one day break free from its origins in the human mind to continue its evolution exclusively through computers, robots, and the like (Moravec 1988:1–5, Kurzweil 1999:253, Rawlins 1997:19–20, 40).

To be sure, information technology continues its development at breathtaking speed, and perhaps in a few years or decades conjectures such as these may not seem as far-fetched as they do today. But by now I hope it is clear that my way of arresting the moving target is to insist that I am not writing about information technology *per se*. My interest is in the implications of information technology for culture and society. Therefore, I will not discuss the most avant-garde research in artificial intelligence, for it does not yet have discernable social consequences. Nor, for the same reason, will I make predictions beyond the very near future. Instead, my analysis is restricted to the applications of artificial intelligence that have become widespread over the past several years. That means talking about automated research services such as WESTLAW and LEXIS, about Internet search engines and keyword searching, and about e-mail, word processing, and other electronic procedures that have become commonplace. These have already had major impacts on the professions, on scientific and humanistic research, and on the way people gather information, communicate, and, as a result of all that, think. Attempting to understand the unintended and rarely recognized social consequences of these current realities is daunting (and rewarding) enough that I, at least, am not tempted to speculate beyond them to what may happen in the more distant future.

Chapter 2

Cultural Contradiction
and Compartmentalization

Not everyone believes that cultural divisiveness and clashes are bad things. Speaking in a venue that might have preferred cultural differences to be celebrated, or at least tolerated—the 1971 UNESCO conference to mark the International Year to Combat Racism and Racial Discrimination— eminent anthropologist Claude Lévi-Strauss said: "It is not at all invidious to place one way of life or thought above all others or to feel little drawn to other values . . . diversity results from the desire of each culture to resist the cultures surrounding it, to distinguish itself from them—in short, to be itself" (Lévi-Strauss 1985:xiv).

Clifford Geertz dismisses any banal celebration of cultural differences as disingenuous, and Lévi-Strauss's ethnocentrism (to name it for what it is) is dangerously idealizing one's own ways while demonizing those of others (Geertz 2000:86). Today's world of intertwined cultural diversity is poorly served by both of them and necessitates, Geertz insists, something akin to a fine-grained ethnographic approach that seeks to understand, in minute particulars, why, from their own point of view, people think and act as they do. Only then will we be able to grasp the relationship of their behavior to our own and on that basis learn to cope successfully with the realities of contemporary life (pp. 82–88).

CULTURE WARS

Geertz is, of course, absolutely right. But beyond the academy and some insular places in social planning and development, Lévi-Strauss's depiction of current realities is accurate. Too often the desire to resist other cultures takes the form of narrow sanctimoniousness, as when Muslim, Christian, and Jewish fundamentalists, convinced that they alone possess God's truth, consider themselves called to champion that truth over other ways of thinking. In such cases cultural differences are perceived as contradictory, and they generate overt hostility. At the extreme, partisans embrace violence as a way to thwart their adversaries, whom they regard with pure hatred. The United States is known in many places as the "great Satan," and members of the Bush administration routinely brand America's adversaries as "evil." Recent events in the Balkans, Rwanda, and Darfur prove that the unbelievable brutality of ethnic cleansing and genocide still haunts the world.

Cultural conflict on the global scale has been legitimated by ethnocentric scholarship. Bernard Lewis (2002) speaks of the exhaustion and decline of Islamic civilization, while Samuel Huntington predicts that "the great divisions among humankind and the dominating source of conflict will be cultural. . . . The clash of civilizations will dominate global politics" (Huntington 1993:22). The reason, thinly masking an assumption of Western superiority, is that "Western ideas of individualism, liberalism, constitutionalism, human rights, equality, liberty, the rule of law, democracy, free markets, the separation of church and state, often have little resonance in Islamic, Confucian, Japanese, Hindu, Buddhist, or Orthodox cultures. Western efforts to propagate such ideas produce instead a reaction against 'human rights imperialism' and a reaffirmation of indigenous values, as can be seen in the support for religious fundamentalism by the younger generation in non-Western cultures" (pp. 40–41).

The divisive, maladapted influence of culture is not played out only on the international stage. Much concern has been vented of late about the polarizing effect of the "culture wars" splitting contemporary society (Hunter 1991, 1994; Hout 1999; Miller and Hoffmann 1999). James Davison Hunter's (1991) eponymous book on the subject stresses differences between agnostics and left-leaning progressive Christians, on the one hand, and the religious right, consisting of conservative Catholics and fundamentalist Protestants, on the other. The newspapers carry reports of clashes between the cultural values of these constituencies on a daily basis.

People are deeply divided over whether the Pledge of Allegiance should include the phrase "under God." Crèches in town squares at Christmas stir up controversy, and in 2003 the chief justice of Alabama was suspended from office for refusing to remove a monument displaying the Ten Commandments from the rotunda of the state judicial center. Other important battlefields are the family, sexuality, and lifestyle, where conflict rages over abortion, gay and lesbian rights, feminism, and the patriarchal family. At the moment, the hot-button issue is same-sex marriage (Toner 2004). States are rushing to adopt constitutional amendments to "defend marriage" by restricting it to a relationship between one man and one woman, and in some cases the homophobia is strong enough to deny legal recognition of same-sex relationships outside of marriage. In public education the battle is joined over prayer in the schools, sex education, and the teaching of evolution. In 1999, a creationist majority on the Kansas State Board of Education voted to deemphasize evolution in the high school curriculum, a measure that was reversed in 2001 after an election changed the composition of the board. Similar moves against evolution have surfaced more recently in Ohio, Texas, Indiana, Alabama, Kansas again, and elsewhere.

Another battlefield for the culture wars is the campus. Conservatives denounce much of the faculty as former hippies and anti-Vietnam War protesters and decry the institutionalization of politically correct speech and behavior on campus as an infringement of freedom of expression. In early 2004, complaints arose on campuses such as the University of Colorado and Brandeis University regarding professors' alleged unfair treatment and threats of poor grades against conservative students, and movements are under way to monitor classes of left-leaning faculty to document political bias. The University of Colorado attracted unwelcome attention again in 2005 and 2006 with highly publicized demands that ethnic studies professor Ward Churchill be fired for referring to victims of the World Trade Center terrorist attack as "little Eichmanns": technocrats who implement the U.S. government's oppressive foreign policy. Conservatives dismiss programs such as women's studies, gay and lesbian studies, African American studies and Native American studies as platforms for liberal propaganda rather than true scholarly inquiry. Liberals demand that courses in cultural traditions other than Western civilization satisfy core graduation requirements and, within Western civilization itself, clamor for requiring texts by women, people of color, and other disenfranchised minorities along with (and, in certain cases, instead of) the "canon" by "DWMs" (dead white males) such as Shakespeare, Rousseau, and the Founding Fathers.

The American political arena is now more viscerally polarized than at any time since the Vietnam War. The right-wing drive to impeach President Clinton over the Monica Lewinsky affair was mean-spirited in the extreme, and the left wing regards President George W. Bush with undisguised animosity for, as they say, stealing the 2000 election, invading Iraq for trumped-up reasons, plunging that country into chaos under the American occupation, and eroding civil liberties at home as part of the "war on terror." On the floor of the U.S. Senate, the vice president of the United States tells a senator of the other party to "go fuck yourself," and afterward says he feels better for having said it (Udargo 2004). Intense polarization between left and right was the hallmark of the 2004 election, with many commentators discussing the country's division between "red states" and "blue states." Bipartisan cooperation in legislatures at the national, state, and even local levels is rare. As applied by figures such as former House Majority Leader Tom DeLay, the political strategy of choice now seems to be for the majority to ram its agenda down the throats of the opposition instead of working together toward a mutually acceptable solution.

Efforts to account for the polarization of American society today include the rise of the religious right, a testy anxiety born of the terrorist attacks of 9/11, and white apprehension about losing dominance to a growing flood of non-white immigrants (a worry also for many Western Europeans). More generally, Edward Tiryakian sees the contemporary conflicts as symptomatic of a return of postmodern society to mechanical solidarity (1994:12–13), a view that resonates with Jan Fernback's observation that "certain religious and cultural interests have retreated to tribalism in the wake of multiculturalism, diversity, and identity politics" (1997:43). Still, the perception that ours is a unique time when culture wars are heating up on every front may not be accurate. Surely Wayne Baker goes too far in asserting that American society is not polarized at all (2005:94), but studies over the short term of a few decades indicate a nuanced picture, where divisiveness may be on the rise over some issues but remains the same or even declines over others (Dimaggio, Evans, and Bryson 1996; Evans 2003). In the longer view, Hunter identifies multiple culture wars in American society going back to the founding of the Republic (1991:35–39, 137, 198–201). European history in the sixteenth and seventeenth centuries is replete with religious conflicts. Disputes between science and religion have raged since the seventeenth century.

The term itself, *Kulturkampf,* was first applied to the antagonism between Protestants and Catholics in Bismarck's Germany more than a century ago (Clark and Kaiser 2003:1). In forms ranging from scholarly debate to all-out war, ideological conflicts between monarchy and democracy dominated political life in the West from the seventeenth century onward, and battles between fascism, communism, and capitalism defined the twentieth century on a global scale. Antagonism between Muslims and Hindus has been rampant for years in South Asia; dissension between Ibo and Yoruba, Hutu and Tutsi, Afars and Issas, Boers and English, Catholics and Protestants, and Blacks and Whites has fomented violent conflict in Nigeria, Rwanda, Djibouti, South Africa, Northern Ireland, and the United States. And all that represents only a tiny fraction of the list. Instead of returning to a state of mechanical solidarity, it seems closer to the mark to say that these manifestations of culture have never left it.

Culture wars erupt then not just here and now but in many times and places. The inescapable conclusion is that they are a systemic component of ideological diversity, whenever and wherever that occurs. This view is consistent with Hunter, who defines "cultural conflict very simply as political and social hostility rooted in different systems of moral understanding . . . [that] always have a character of ultimacy to them. They are . . . basic commitments and beliefs that provide a source of identity, purpose, and togetherness for the people who live by them" (1991:42).

Three obvious generalizations about the culture wars should be highlighted. First, they are *cultural* because they are grounded in ideologies and values, what Hunter calls "systems of moral understanding." Second, they are *wars* because of the ultimate nature of these moral or cultural systems. When the principles defining people's "identity, purpose, and togetherness" are on the line, they are not about to dilute them in order to get along with other people who espouse opposing principles. Third, no one (except those who welcome imminent Armageddon and the end of the world) thinks culture wars are a good thing. They are clearly detrimental to the overall harmony of society, and it would be better for people individually and for society generally if there were less polarizing conflict. It does not follow from this that everything cultural is bad, but it does support the contention of the preceding chapter that culture has come to exercise a divisive, detrimental influence in contemporary society.

The differences at stake in the culture wars are contradictory. What of the other negative form of difference that we have identified, compartmentalization? This describes those situations where the beliefs and actions of different individuals or groups do not so much come into open conflict with each other as coexist in relative isolation. I think the default position of the great majority of people toward other cultures is indifference. They harbor no outspoken animosity toward other cultures, nor do they manifest much interest in them. They simply take it for granted that their own way is the right way and what is happening elsewhere is not particularly relevant. As I write this, for example, the Kansas Board of Education is debating whether to diminish the already minimal attention given to foreign countries in the public schools social studies curriculum in order to devote more time to American and Kansas history. Even in this time of anxiety about terrorism, unilateral American foreign policy, preemptive war, and the lowest standing in memory of the United States in the eyes of the rest of the world, most people seem to think that what happens elsewhere is of scant interest or importance. It is a prime example of what I have called compartmental difference.

Compartmentalization, which traffics more in indifference than in altercation, appears to be more benign than contradiction. At one point, however, Durkheim implied that compartmentalization has even more insidious consequences than contradiction (1933:371–73). He held that the callous disregard of the effect of overly routinized work on the assembly line worker is a "debasement of human nature" that reduces the individual to "an inert piece of machinery" (p. 371). Another example of how compartmental difference debases human beings, and one that merits more extended treatment, is the current view of poverty in the United States.

POVERTY: FROM MAKING A DIFFERENCE
TO INDIFFERENCE

At earlier stages in its history certain meanings were associated with poverty which, if they did not necessarily ease the plight of the poor, they at least provided explanations of their condition and delineated what could be done about it.[1] The rugged individualist view of poverty that dominated the late eighteenth and nineteenth centuries held that the poor themselves, because of their ignorance, indolence, and unrestrained reproduction, were responsible for their miserable condition. The solution proposed by Malthus was to educate them. Once they realized that the cause of their poverty was their own profligate reproduction, most of them would mend their ways. This would have the multiple salutary effects of enabling present paupers to escape their poverty, preventing young people from falling into it, and turning them all into more productive citizens as they bring their animal drives under rational control (Malthus 1992:228, 259–66, 274–77, 328). These meanings provided an understanding of poverty as a blight on civilized society, and they pointed out what needed to be done to abolish it. The image of what could be accomplished motivated many of the non-poor to dedicate themselves to reforming the poor with something akin to missionary zeal.

Again, the state welfare view of poverty that prevailed through much of the twentieth century contained its own meanings that, while very different from those of rugged individualism, also accounted for the cause of poverty and charted a clear course of action for dealing with it. On this view, poverty is not the fault of the poor but is the product of a deeply flawed socioeconomic system. Hence, the solution is to reform the system. This too was a goal to which many devoted themselves at considerable cost. It asks those in privileged positions to forfeit some of their fortune for the sake of a more equitable distribution of wealth. It requires massive effort and expenditures by society at large to provide equal opportunity for all. And it might even demand the sacrifice of partisans' lives in a violent Marxist revolution.

Meanings such as these are absent from prevailing views of poverty today. To be sure, the notion that destitute dependence erodes the character while responsible self-sufficiency bolsters it remains. It manifests itself in annoyance and impatience with people who cannot get and hold a job, or who as unmarried teenagers place no restraint on their sexuality and take no responsibility for the children they produce. However, these sentiments are seldom linked any more to some transcendent crusade such as saving souls or creating a truly equal and just society, or with any notion that the voluntary, rational government of our natural instincts spurs the upward growth of civilization. Expression of greed and instant self-gratification is at least as popular (and far more attainable) among the rich these days as it is among the poor.

The difference emerges from a comparison of Charles Murray's contemporary proposal (1984) to end public welfare with the ideas proposed by Malthus nearly two centuries ago. Malthus's convictions about the value of controlling base passions and social progress are embedded primarily in his desire to educate the poor, and this part of his program Murray does not recapitulate. Indeed, where Malthus believed that the poor could escape their poverty if they were educated, Murray colludes with Richard Herrnstein in the very different view that education cannot help lower-class people very much, because their innate intelligence is limited (Herrnstein and Murray 1994). In this sense Murray's view is leaner and meaner than rugged individualism, for it sees fewer prospects for the poor to improve their state. And herein lies a cop-out for the rest of society. Since the mentally slow poor are unlikely to benefit from better education, we are justified in declining to allocate the resources to provide it for them.

The contemporary view of poverty is born of frustration with the failure of state welfare initiatives to dent the problem of poverty. Communism did not work, liberal welfare states are being forced to roll back their social benefits, and in the United States, after decades of dashed hopes and expenditures that have produced no tangible benefits, the nation seems tacitly to have acknowledged that we fought a war on poverty, and poverty won (see Sawhill 1988:1085). Defeated, people have lost the hope that they can do much about poverty. Not because the obstacles seem more difficult to surmount than in previous epochs; in fact, the very difficulty of taking appropriate action regarding poverty challenged people of earlier periods to devote themselves wholeheartedly to the task. The problem is that, today, no appropriate course of action relative to poverty is apparent at all. As a result, the motivation to commitment and self-sacrifice in the cause of combating poverty has gone slack, and large numbers of the non-poor have withdrawn from the arena entirely. Unmotivated to grapple with a problem for which they can discern no solution, the non-poor increasingly find it more bearable to compartmentalize poverty, to hide it away so that they do not have to think about it at all. This importantly includes positioning themselves so that they rarely encounter poverty by ordering where they live (in gated communities), where their children go to school (private ones), what they read, and what they expose themselves to in such a way that poor people intrude minimally upon their lives and consciousness.

Actually, this strategy does entail a solution of sorts to the problem of poverty, and a remarkably clean and cheap solution at that. It makes poverty disappear by the simple expedient of not acknowledging it. As poverty theorist Michael Katz recognized, poverty is not so much the existence of poor people as the prevailing discourse about them (1989:7–8). Becoming indifferent to poverty may not alter its statistical incidence, but it does alter how it is conceptualized, and *that* is the decisive factor in determining what is done (or, more to the point, not done) about it. If people will just stop worrying and thinking and talking about it, then poverty will disappear. There will still be poor *people*, of course, but as their plight is compartmentalized and ignored, the grim reality of their lives disappears from public awareness, and the social problem of poverty is solved.

But such a solution has its cost. In situations such as this one, compartmental difference is even more detrimental than contradiction. The clash of opposing values and opinions may tear at the bonds of social solidarity, but at least it involves a certain vitality in that people deeply care about certain things and are willing to express themselves forcefully, and to work and sacrifice to achieve their objectives. The compartmentalization of poverty brings about a debilitating condition that is akin to what Robert Jay Lifton (1979) would call psychic numbing. This is a coping mechanism that sets in when things seem so horrendous or so insoluble that it is safer simply to act as if they did not exist. It can be considered a form of denial, or it can be seen as a case of human beings constructing or inventing reality to suit themselves. In either event, it involves indifference to the undeniably real suffering of other human beings. And that, as Durkheim might well say, is a debasement of human nature.

THE DIVISIVE EFFECTS OF AUTOMATION

Most of what will be said in this book about the automation of information has to do with how it acts as an antidote to the trouble with culture, diminishing divisiveness by encouraging a view of cultural differences as complementary rather than contradictory or compartmental. This position may come as something of a surprise, for the more general opinion is probably that automation can be and often is used for the opposite end of magnifying contradictory and compartmental differences (Becker and Wehner 2001). From that perspective, automation exacerbates rather than ameliorates the trouble with culture. This view of the matter must not be ignored. I will discuss it now, saving the other side for later chapters.

People often use the greatly expanded opportunities that automation provides for getting information, communicating and forming relationships in a highly focused manner, zeroing in on precisely what they already know they want. Consider television. It began as a broadcast medium consisting of a few networks, each of which provided a general range of offerings to a large and diverse audience. Today, as cable and satellite technologies greatly increase the number of available channels, television is transforming into a narrowcast medium where not just individual programs but whole networks are devoted to special topics such as news, comedy, history, sports, cooking, Roman Catholicism, and many more. This is especially conducive to compartmental difference, for it is now possible to watch television programs tailored to one's special interests all day long, with no interference from any competing information.

Another major source of customized information is the Internet. In addition to Web sites on every imaginable topic, computer-mediated communication enables people to make their own contributions to ongoing discussions. This takes a variety of forms. E-mail and innumerable discussion groups or "list-servs" link people with common intellectual and other interests. The Usenet, beginning in 1979 at the University of North Carolina as a connection between just two computers, by 1999 spanned the globe and enabled millions of people to exchange information in over 14,300 newsgroups or discussion forums on any number of topics (Smith 1999:196–97). Text chat (also called Internet Relay Chat) and MUDs (multi-user domains) allow people to interact directly, in synchronous communication. Many Web sites also support visitors' asynchronous or synchronous interaction (Kollock and Smith 1999:6–8), as do numerous blogs. More than 80,000 topic-oriented collective discussion groups were in existence on the Internet as a whole by April 4, 1998. That was more than triple the number identified on January 27, 1996 (Wellman and Gulia 1999:172), and doubtless the present number is much larger still. All this too feeds compartmental differences, as some people interact almost exclusively with others who share their narrow interests.

Many cybercommunities represent an extreme form of narrowcasting especially conducive to both compartmental and contradictory difference. Religious fundamentalists, survivalists, gun enthusiasts, racists, peaceniks, tree huggers, and others can easily find like-minded individuals and groups on the Internet, and they can saturate themselves with the only kind of information they want. As Bill Machrone (1996:85) put it, "The good news is that people with specific interests can find lots of similar-minded people with whom to interact. The bad news is that people whose behavior already tends toward the antisocial will likely find increased support for their tendencies, unmoderated by interaction with the rest of the world. . . . [T]here [is] the potential for the weird to get weirder." This kind of compartmentalization often fuels contradictory difference when the intentional myopia reinforces people's conviction that their view of the world is the only correct one, and that they must take action to defend and promulgate it. The virulence of contradictory differences between some persuasions locked in culture wars is easy to perceive by listening to their rhetoric or glancing at their Web sites. Among the most venomous of these are sites extolling white supremacy, such as http://www.volker-mord.com, http://aryan-nations.org/, and http://www.creativitymove-ment.us.

People who participate together in computer-mediated discussion groups constitute new kinds of social entities. A good deal of debate has been devoted to how they resemble and differ from other kinds of communities (e.g. Postman 1992; Rheingold 1993; Keeble and Loader 2001; S. G. Jones 1995, 1997; Poster 1997; Smith and Kollock 1999). The technology of the Internet enables these groups to escape the limitations of space to include members from any part of the world. Although professional and academic associations have crossed national boundaries by means of their symposia and journals for decades, automation has greatly expanded and accelerated this as interest groups of all descriptions, in the popular as well as the professional culture, take shape and flourish in that unbounded and instantly traversed region known as cyberspace.

Some people embrace their electronic communities wholeheartedly. Howard Rheingold (1993) enthuses over the intimacy and mutual concern that in his view mark online interaction among members of the WELL (Whole Earth 'Lectronic Link). While researching donor insemination a few years ago, I visited a Web-based discussion group devoted to that topic. Contributors consisted of women who had children, or were trying to have them, by donor insemination. Most of their messages dealt with efforts, experiences, and advice regarding the technique, but more general accounts also appeared about their children's activities, attitudes of relatives and friends, problems at work, vacation trips, and so on. I was struck by the warmth and generosity of the responses that the various postings evoked.

The question, of course, is whether sitting alone at a computer terminal and tapping out supportive sentiments to people one has never met is equivalent to the investment of emotional and material resources required to sustain face-to-face relationships or to belong to traditional communities. Sherry Turkle reports: "Women and men tell me that the rooms and mazes on MUDs are safer than city streets, virtual sex is safer than sex anywhere, MUD friendships are more intense than real ones, and when things don't work out you can always leave" (1995:244). How the intensity of MUD friendships fits is unclear, but the ease of leaving implies that experience in cybercommunities is attenuated and commitment to them is contingent. Leaving is an option that seems to be exercised frequently. Marc Smith's research, for example, revealed that 42% of Usenet newsgroups had less than 100 messages posted in a ten-week period, while another 20% were completely inactive (1999:203).[2]

Human interaction in cybercommunities has a number of peculiarities. It occurs at a distance, with a time delay in communities that use asynchronous communication. It is observed by unknown numbers of "lurkers," who do not contribute, whose presence is invisible, and who can scarcely be considered community members. Many of those who do contribute are only loosely constrained by the rules of "Netiquette," and some of them remain anonymous or present themselves disingenuously. Membership in many cybercommunities hinges upon nothing more than frequent visits to the newsgroup or Web site. This minimal commitment leads some commentators to doubt that these groups are communities in any meaningful sense of the word. Members of a true community, they point out, acknowledge an obligation to it as a body and to each other as individuals as well as expressing an interest in it. Whether it takes the form of an affirmation of faith or belief, a moral imperative guiding conduct, or support with time and money, communities demand something tangible from their members. Most cybercommunities, on the other hand, are composed of people who share a common interest but assume little or nothing in the way of community responsibilities (Willson 1997; Gurak 1997:8–11; Fernback 1997:45; Watson 1997:122–24; Becker and Wehner 2001:80). Joining is a matter of signing up for the list-serv, or opening the Usenet group or Web site when one feels inclined to do so. The group has no claims on its members. It is a far cry from the membership requirements of training, apprenticeship, initiation rituals, swearing of oaths, payment of dues, holding office, and other obligations that more traditional groups have placed on their members. Nor do members have any tangible claim on each other. If one feels others are making undue demands, the fact that the relationship is grounded in electronic communication makes it easy to break it off simply by no longer replying to messages or visiting the site.

Furthermore, the range of operation of cybergroups is sharply curtailed. Activities that are commonplace with traditional groups—face-to-face meetings, private or public programs, paid professional staff, fund-raising, constructing buildings or physical centers for conducting their work—are rare among cybercommunities. Their main function is internal communication. Joint projects consist of little more than e-mail-writing campaigns in support of causes they espouse. One needs only to compare cybergroups with churches, labor unions, civic music or theater groups, Mafia families, political parties, Masonic lodges, and any number of other traditional groups to realize how different they are.

To summarize, electronic communities are more flexible in every sense than traditional ones. They are numerous and varied enough to satisfy virtually any interest, and they have no geographical restrictions. They are easy to join and easy to leave, and they make minimal demands on their members. Deep bonds of commitment to the group and friendship and trust among its members are rarely forged in such an environment.

Another form of social connection—networking—is also affected by automation. Unlike a group, which is a relatively bounded plurality of persons who interact for certain purposes more intensively with each other than with outsiders, a network consists of the set of relationships centering on each individual (friends, relatives, work associates, others). The networks of some people (such as husband and wife) overlap considerably, but they are never isomorphic. Networks of relatives (anthropologists often call those "kindreds") and friends have always existed, but automation has made it easier to form and maintain them because telephone and e-mail technologies facilitate instant communication over vast distances (Wellman 2001). It is useful, however, to distinguish how automation affects generalized and focused relationships in networks. (Focused relationships are those where the parties share only one or a narrow range of interests; generalized ones are between individuals such as relatives and close personal friends who have a general interest in each other's activities and well-being.) Electronic communication is effective for maintaining generalized relationships that began with personal interaction when people are later separated by geographical distance. But networking relationships that begin with and remain limited to automated communication tend to be focused—limited to specific issues and interests. They parallel those among members of cybergroups in this, and for the same reason: the automated environment offers less opportunity than face-to-face contact for individuals to take an interest in the different facets of each other's lives. This is especially true of e-mail, where the visual and audible contact that stimulates broader interest between interlocutors is absent. Even in chat rooms, which more closely simulate generalized interpersonal conversation, uncertainties about the other's motivations and ingenuousness inhibit the formation of close personal ties. The main exceptions to this are those automated contacts initiated expressly to explore the possibility of forming generalized relationships, such as computer dating services. Instructively, however, people do not normally think that such a generalized relationship can be truly established until they go beyond purely electronic communication and begin to interact in person.

The narrowly focused concerns of both cybercommunities and automated networks afford new possibilities for the expression of contradictory and compartmental differences by enabling like-minded people to immerse themselves in information and associations that support their preconceived interests and biases. This is how automation provides a new opportunity for the preestablished categories and received truths associated with culture to express themselves. Used in this focused way, automation exacerbates the trouble with culture by linking up large numbers of closed-minded people who share the same values and understandings and who further contradictory differences by denouncing alternative ones, or compartmental differences by saturating themselves in their own ways of thinking and behaving to the exclusion of everything else.

It is necessary, however, to recognize a certain pallor in automated expressions of culture when compared to its more embodied forms. E-mail distributed news from Citizens for Legitimate Government, MoveOn, or Truthout reinforces the anti-war, anti-Bush administration biases of those who receive it, but those who limit themselves to that are less likely to have an impact on national politics than those who attend meetings, sponsor forums and lectures, participate in protest demonstrations, work for candidates, or run for office. White supremacists may be reassured in their beliefs by visiting Web sites such as http://www.aryan-nations.org, but if that is all they do, then they will make less of a difference than those who also live in a community dedicated to those beliefs, attend the annual rallies of the Ku Klux Klan in Smackover, Arkansas, or go out and lynch someone. Purely electronic groups and relationships are narrower and shallower than face-to-face ones, easier to form or join, easier to dissolve or leave, and less likely to produce committed action.

Finally, although automation certainly can be enlisted for the narrow, reinforcing ends we have been discussing, nothing about it requires that. All of the media and organizational forms just considered—television, e-mail, chat groups, MUDs, list-servs, cybergroups, cybernetworks—are also used to broaden perspectives, to gain exposure to new ideas, and to seek constructive, complementary relationships among cultural differences. Such an open-minded attitude is expected of scholars, students, attorneys, and others who use automated resources for educational or professional purposes. It also characterizes recreational users who surf the Net or interact with each other out of sheer curiosity.

The following chapters highlight certain intrinsic characteristics of automation that support and encourage these open-minded attitudes more than preautomated techniques of information management ever could. Recognizing what these characteristics are will enable us to understand just how automation holds a unique potential to ease the trouble with culture.

Chapter 3

Fixing the Trouble with Culture
Relativism, Postmodernism, and Automation

If culture has become divisive in contemporary society, then the question is, can a solution be found? Is there something that can bring about a shift from the disruption, conflict, or indifference that comes from seeing cultural differences as contradictory or compartmental to the more constructive, cooperative condition that comes from seeing cultural differences as complementary? Durkheim thought this would come about automatically, as increasing division of labor and social complexity "enfeeble" culture (1933:170), rendering it more general and indeterminate, with greater room for individual differences (p. 172). But the previous chapter has demonstrated that far from weakening culture, the more common outcome is for contradictory and compartmental differences to intensify as different cultures stake their territories more stridently within and between large, heterogeneous societies in a shrinking world.

Nonetheless, there is a sense in which Durkheim was correct in thinking that the solution lies in culture becoming "enfeebled," although I prefer "open." If cultural premises become less dogmatic, then it becomes possible for people to get some distance on them, to regard them more rationally, critically, and dispassionately. This enables them to realize that their own cultural principles often complement those of others rather than contradicting or being incommensurable with them. But since, contra Durkheim, this cannot be expected to happen automatically with the complex division of labor, some other mechanism to open culture must be sought. For James Davison Hunter, the best hope boils down to tolerance and a quest for mutual understanding. Citizens should be educated to be able to understand the contexts and meanings that ground divergent points of view, and then they should sit down and thrash out their differences in a civil manner in an effort to find common ground (Hunter 1994:231–39).

This sounds reasonable enough, but it does not grapple with the crucial issue of how to get people into the frame of mind to be able to engage in such tolerant and constructive debate. It seems to me that three candidates present themselves. Two—cultural relativism and postmodernism—are theoretical or philosophical ways of looking at things. We shall see that their prospects of success are not encouraging, largely because it is extremely difficult to get people to change their ways of thinking by directly appealing to them to do so. The third—the automation of information—is more promising. A technological innovation, it was not explicitly designed to open culture. But precisely that is one of its many unintended consequences. This chapter will first address why relativism and postmodernism have failed to garner widespread allegiance and then explore of the sociocultural ramifications of automation.

CULTURAL RELATIVISM

The intentional effort to view cultural differences rationally and as complementary has come to be a hallmark of my own field of anthropology. Early in its history, in thrall to the theory of unilineal evolutionism, anthropology itself could fairly be called an instrument of closed culture. It reinforced the superiority of one culture by purporting to demonstrate how various extant societies of the world represented lower rungs on an evolutionary ladder that culminated in the anthropologists' own, late-nineteenth-century Euroamerican culture. But in the twentieth century, anthropology took a decidedly different turn. Virtually all developments in the field—the Boasian approach, functionalism, structuralism, post-structuralism, ecological anthropology, cultural materialism, symbolic or interpretive anthropology—have made it a point to refrain from denigrating other cultures, from charging them with error or scant progress, or claiming that our own culture is superior to them.[1] The goal has rather been to appreciate other cultures and, in most cases, to understand them in their own terms. This means that criteria for understanding and evaluating that are operative in one culture should not be used to judge what happens in another culture, nor are there any absolute criteria that apply to all cultures. The truth of propositions about the activities of witches, the efficacy of prayer, the behavior of subatomic particles, or the morality of killing strangers, beating wives, or marrying first cousins all depends on the standards reigning in the culture in which such things are said or done. This roughly (and there are many nuanced versions of it) is the general orientation known as cultural relativism.

The relativist perspective is often helpful when encountering cultural beliefs and behaviors radically different from our own. Consider the Hua of highland Papua New Guinea. Adults in that society are in the habit of wiping their bodily products on small children. A man, pausing in the midst of some exerting work, may take some of his perspiration in his hand and rub it over his little son or nephew. Bodily oil and vomit are used in the same way, and eating, drinking, or otherwise coming into contact with other people's feces, blood, saliva, and urine, under proper circumstances, is thought to stimulate growth or cure disease (Meigs 1984:109–10). If that were not enough, when an adult dies the body is consumed by the descendants. The Hua believe that if a person does not eat the corpse of one's same-sex parent, then "that person and his or her children, animals, and crops will become stunted and weak" (p. 110).

Anthropologist Anna Meigs explains these curious customs in terms of the Hua concept of *nu*. Understood as the vital essence or life force, *nu* inheres in the body, and vestiges of it are found in all bodily excreta. Hua adults rub their perspiration and other body products on small children in order to transmit *nu* to them, thus helping them grow vital and strong. The funeral cannibalism completes the process. Consumption of the decedent's flesh marks the final step in the transfer of *nu* from senior to junior. These ideas also explain the Hua notion of aging. *Nu* is finite, so giving it to others depletes one's own supply. Years of excreting bodily substances take their toll. One's energy declines, the other symptoms of aging appear, and, when the *nu* finally drops below a critical threshold, death ensues (pp. 119–21).

Anthropologists take a relativist stance in order to grasp the rationale behind alien beliefs and practices by considering them "in their own terms." Doing so often reveals that even customs as exotic and initially off-putting as those of the Hua complement those of other cultures. Such is the case with the difference between the Hua and our non-wiping, non-cannibalistic selves. When we understand the meaning behind the Hua customs, we realize that we can learn something from them, and they can learn something from us. For many in our society, death carries a dreadful finality about it, at least as far as earthly existence is concerned. When one dies, one disappears from the earth, and that is the end of it. For the Hua, human beings are temporary vessels of *nu*, which waxes and wanes in each individual as it makes its way through the generations. Thus the life force neither begins with the individual's birth nor ends with death. Translating *nu* into what is important about life for us—principles to live by, aspiration toward achievement, the importance of relationships with family and friends—we can learn from the Hua that the bookends of life are not so ultimate. Those values live beyond us in both directions: we acquire them from those who preceded us, and we transmit them to those who come after. Similarly, the Hua can learn from us that one is not diminished by transferring a valuable part of oneself to someone else. On the contrary, those who pass knowledge, moral standards, and models for successful living to the next generation are themselves enlivened in the process. Thus these two very different cultural ways of looking at life have something to offer each other. The understanding that comes from taking them both together is deeper than that provided by either of them alone.

The trouble with culture would be much alleviated if people in general were to adopt cultural relativism. Then they would achieve a better understanding of other cultural values and institutions, which would allow them to perceive such differences as often complementary to their own. This would greatly diminish levels of intolerance, conflict, and indifference between cultures. But I do not think mass acceptance of cultural relativism is likely to occur anytime soon. Relativism is an extremely controversial subject over which a great deal of ink has been spilled by philosophers and social scientists. This is not the place for an exhaustive review of the criticisms of relativism, but I will mention a few of them to support my claim that relativism is unlikely to capture the hearts and minds of the masses.

For one thing, relativism is often accused of being either incoherent or self-contradictory. The relativist claims: "There are no absolutely or universally true propositions; they are all relative." The critic then asks, "What about the proposition you just made, about there being no absolutely or universally true propositions? Is *that* absolutely or universally true?" To remain consistent, the relativist would have to answer, "No, the proposition that there are no absolutely and universally true propositions is a proposition like any other. It is not absolutely and universally true; it too is relative." But to say that is to abandon the core proposition of relativism, leaving one mystified as to what relativism can mean. If, on the other hand, the relativist replies in the affirmative, claiming that the proposition that there are no absolutely or universally true propositions is itself absolutely or universally true, then he contradicts himself by granting that there is at least one absolutely and universally true proposition.

Since even people with the same culture are not unanimous on everything, one could argue that relativism should be extended to the claim that the truth of propositions varies among individuals. That position, which Michael Lynch calls "simple relativism," is even more clearly vulnerable to the accusation of self-contradiction or incoherence. He writes:

> Suppose I am such a relativist and announce that there is no such thing as truth *per se*, there is only truth-for-me or truth-for-you. A fair question to ask would be whether the statement I just made is true or just true-for-me. If I say that relativism is simply true, then I have apparently contradicted myself. For if relativism is true (for everyone, as it were) then it is false—it is not true that *all* truth is relative. On the other hand, if I go the other way and say that relativism is only true relative to me, I am consistent but unable to convince anyone who doesn't already agree with me. You need only remark that relativism is not true for you. (Lynch 2004:32–33, emphasis in original)

Another common criticism of relativism is that it requires belief in everything, or in nothing. The version of it that is particularly susceptible to this objection has been phrased by Richard Rorty: "'Relativism' is the view that every belief on a certain topic, or perhaps about *any* topic, is as good as every other" (Rorty 1982:166, emphasis in original). Rorty goes on to say that "No one holds this view." And no wonder. If every belief is as good as another, then why believe anything? But that nihilistic reading seems closer to relativism's close cousin postmodernism, so we will defer addressing it for a moment.

The other possibility—that if one belief is as good as another, then one should affirm all beliefs—is fairly close to the relativist's view that every belief should be evaluated in its own terms. But then one would have to say that astrology is as true as astronomy, alchemy as reasonable as chemistry, and voodoo medicine as good as what they teach at Johns Hopkins. The problem, of course, is that there comes a point for everyone where they simply cannot refrain from judging what is done in other cultures by the standards of their own culture. Where this point lies varies along a continuum running from people who are ethnocentric as a matter of course and dismiss other cultures without much thought, to those who are keenly interested in other cultures and want to view them openly and sympathetically. In what amounts to a caricature of the ethnocentric pole, on the last day of an introductory course in cultural anthropology a young coed sweetly asked me, "But Dr. Hanson, if the Chinese *know* about spoons and forks, why do they keep using chopsticks?" I had the urge to resign then and there, although perhaps (I devoutly hope) she was pulling my leg. Ethnocentrism at that level is just silly, but it becomes more serious as the differences involved pertain to issues of existential import. How can one continue to believe that a husband should go before and guide his wife in all things and yet affirm the view that women's rights should be equal to men's? What value might people who think that the earth is spherical and revolves around the sun find in ideas that the earth is flat, or that all the heavenly bodies rotate around it? How can someone who is convinced that homosexuality is a sin see merit in the view that gay marriages should be legitimated? How can one hold to the principle that innocent people should not be killed or maimed and still endorse the ancient Aztec practice of large-scale human sacrifice, or clitoridectomy and infibulation (cutting away parts of the labia and suturing them together so that the vaginal orifice is closed to about the size of a pencil) in the Horn of Africa,[2] or the mourning practices of the Dani of West Papua, who, when a family member dies, cut off little girls' fingers at the joints with a stone axe? Practically speaking, cultural relativism does make valuable inroads against narrow-mindedness by encouraging tolerance of differences. But thoroughgoing relativism, as it is generally viewed and criticized, is simply unrealistic. It asks people to accept too much.[3]

POSTMODERNISM

Another trend toward opening culture is the general intellectual movement that has developed over the last few decades under the name postmodernism. It too takes a relativistic perspective that things are not true or false or good or bad in their own right but only in the context of some more general set of assumptions that are themselves not absolute but historically and culturally variable. Postmodernism develops that position further with the notion of radical indeterminacy, which can be traced to the latter twentieth century's "linguistic turn" in philosophy and other branches of scholarship. In the 1920s Swiss linguist Ferdinand de Saussure noted that words and other linguistic signs refer not to things in the world but to concepts. "Dog" refers not to actual canine creatures but to an idea people have regarding such creatures. This may seem like nothing more than an added step: the word may not refer to the creatures, but the word refers to an idea that, in its turn, concerns the creatures. Roughly half a century later, however, authors such as Jacques Derrida, Umberto Eco, and Jean Baudrillard began to argue that linguistic signs refer to other linguistic signs in an infinite sequence of references, and never to things in external reality. From this perspective, language and knowledge are self-referential, closed systems. Propositions regarding what is true, moral, beautiful, or any other judgment are grounded only in other propositions.

This may seem radical, but actually people have been operating in this manner for centuries. Think of the common practice of looking up a word in a dictionary. Every word is defined exclusively in terms of other words. It is a prime example of linguistic signs referring to other linguistic signs, which in their turn refer to still other linguistic signs, ad infinitum. The postmodernist contribution is to raise questions about the relation of such systems of signs to external reality and seriously to entertain the possibility that there may be none at all.

Postmodernism poses a strong challenge to closed culture. That flourishes in an environment of clarity, certainty, permanence, and consensus: when people know very well what they believe, are convinced that those beliefs describe the fixed and permanent nature of the world, and commit themselves unreservedly to them. Postmodernism, with its claim that beliefs refer only to other beliefs, traffics in indeterminacy, contingency, and the constant flux of cross-references. Clearly this has the potential to open culture. Postmodernist fluidity and indeterminacy, if accepted, would move people to realize that no culture has a lock on absolute truth. This realization would make them more flexible and open-minded. That would better equip them to see the merits of other cultures and, therefore, to recognize the complementary relationships that may exist between those cultures and their own. As Kenneth Gergen put it, postmodernism's self-referential, relational view of language,

> do[es] not mean we must abandon empirical research or deliberations
> on the good. . . . Postmodernist thought . . . operates as an invitation to
> reflexivity, encouraging one to consider all propositional realities and
> dictates as local, provisional, and political. Thus, in the case of research,
> there is nothing about postmodern thought that argues against contin-

uing research, for example, on gene splicing, depression, or the effects of day care programs on developing children. . . . However, what postmodern thought does discourage is the reification of the languages used by the communities of scientists conducting such research. It militates against the dissemination of this language as "true" beyond the communities that speak in these particular ways. It invites consideration of the limitations of the local language (what does it exclude?), the potentials inherent in alternative perspectives, and the sociocultural ramifications of both the research and the manner in which it is framed. . . . By much the same token, postmodern thought does not discourage moral deliberation. In many cases, talk of ethics, justice, or rights may have a strong persuasive impact; often it permits pause in a process that might otherwise end in bloodshed. (Gergen 1994:414)

By this reasoning, adopting postmodernist thought would relax cultural dogmas to the point where they would not cause so much trouble, and the world would be a better place for it.

But, alas, postmodernism has not been widely accepted. As has been indicated already, critics claim that its emphasis on indeterminacy and uncertainty dissolves all standards or criteria against which beliefs may be measured and actions evaluated, thus undercutting any foundation upon which one might affirm something, or dissent against anything (Zerzan 1994). It even removes grounds for feelings of alienation, because it disallows any concept of a natural or original condition from which we have become alienated (p. 110). Depriving people of anchors for their beliefs and behavior leaves them adrift in helplessness and hopelessness. It is a pathological condition of anomie and nihilism, where nothing matters and anything goes. People have no reason to follow one moral code rather than another, or, indeed, to follow any moral code at all (see Lindholm 1997). And, indeed, certain postmodernist writers do seem to embrace such nihilism explicitly. The name Jean Baudrillard often turns up in this context. With reference to the countdown to 2000, in just one of many passages expressing his belief that contemporary culture has come to a state of utter exhaustion, he wrote: "We have nothing else now but objects in which not to believe" (1998:3).

Postmodernist nihilism may have a corrosive effect on the self. Psychiatrist Robert Jay Lifton writes: "I have come to see that the older version of personal identity, at least insofar as it suggests inner stability and sameness, was derived from a vision of a traditional culture in which relationships to symbols and institutions are still relatively intact—hardly the case in the last years of the 20th century" (1993:4–5). The breakdown of those relationships has transformed the self into an unstable being that he calls "protean" (pp. 8, 14–24). We shall see later that Lifton regards the protean self in a generally positive light, but he does identify certain pathologies to which it is peculiarly susceptible. "Negative proteanism . . . is fluidity so lacking in moral content and sustainable inner form that it is likely to result in fragmentation (or near fragmentation) of the self, harm to others, or both" (pp. 190–91). "The fragmented self is radically bereft of coherence and continuity, an extreme expression of dissociation" (p. 202); its most severe pathological form may be multiple personality disorder (p. 210).

For all of these reasons, postmodernism has had no more success than relativism in attracting a wide following. Neither has been able to defeat their common adversaries, absolutism and ethnocentrism. It is a pity, because these are the bastions of closed culture and closed minds. Absolutism holds that absolute truth, morality, beauty, and other standards really do exist, and that, going about it in the proper way, it is possible to know what they are. The key phrase here is "going about it in the proper way." Typically this means "going about it in my way." That links absolutism to ethnocentrism, which holds that one's own culture provides exclusive access to what the absolutes are. The ethnocentric person judges other people's beliefs and behavior by one's own cultural standards and, when they come up short by that measure, condemns them as false or pernicious. This is the stuff of the trouble with culture.

The reason cultural relativism and postmodernism have not been more potent forces for opening culture, I think, is because their assault has been too frontal. They have directly challenged the fundamental pillars of culture: clarity, certainty, permanence, and consensus. This threatens the sense of order and stability of those people (and they are in the great majority) who have lived their whole lives taking the tenets of their cultures for granted. Cultural relativism and postmodernism ask them to abandon the anchors of their existence, which is more than they are willing to do. They resist vigorously, often with a sense of outrage. Although the two doctrines are similar enough that both of them may be accused of both failings, we might say that if relativism's urging that every belief be judged by its own cultural contexts asks too much of people, then postmodernism's nihilistic effect on all beliefs and values offers them too little.[4]

AUTOMATION

Another force of a very different sort also opposes closed culture. This is the automation of information. It may seem curious to discuss it in the same breath as relativism and postmodernism because, unlike them, it is not a theory or a philosophical stance. Instead, it is a brute fact of contemporary technology. Yet Karl Marx, V. Gordon Childe, Leslie White, Marvin Harris, and many other scholars hold that roots of significant social change are more likely to be found in the material conditions of life than in the realm of ideas. That is where, often as a result of some technological innovation, people begin to do things differently without thinking a great deal about it. Transformations of habitual behavior then foment change in other areas of life: social and political organization, religion and ideology. Think of the far-reaching ramifications that came in the wake of technological innovations such as the domestication of plants and animals, the smelting of iron, gunpowder, the printing press, the steam engine, automobiles, and the telephone and television, to name just a few.

Although lacking all strategic coordination with them, automation is a natural ally of relativism and postmodernism in the struggle against closed culture. No one intended it, and most people do not even notice it, but I will argue that, advancing from its technological base, automation is prying culture open in a way that is more subtle and yet more effective than relativism and postmodernism. There can be no question that the introduction of computers has made a huge difference in people's lives. Tasks that used to take hours can now be achieved in minutes or even seconds. Cut-and-paste editing of a manuscript is accomplished with a few rapid swipes of the cursor, checkbooks virtually balance themselves by simply marking which payments and deposits have been transacted, and totals are automatically recalculated by changing the amounts in various funds and spreadsheets. E-mail has revolutionized communication. Letters that used to arrive in days by "snail mail" now reach their destinations in instants. It is as easy to send a message to two, ten, or 1,000 recipients as it is to one. With its newsgroups and Web sites, the Internet delivers massive amounts of information on any subject directly to one's desktop or laptop. Business and industry of every description, from airline reservations and banking to universities, wineries, and X-ray laboratories, have become so dependent on automation that they are unable to function when their computer systems go down.

So dramatic is the shift that it is often said that we are living through an information revolution, that this is the age of information (Castells 1997:360–61, 1998:336–37, 2000:509). This entails more than doing the same kind of things we used to do, only faster, easier, and more powerfully. Automated information management is substantially changing human life in many ways, most of which are still poorly understood and many not even recognized. The one I want to highlight is its function as an antidote to the trouble with culture. In a nonconfrontational but inexorable fashion, the automated management of information opens culture by fostering a way of thinking and acting that is conducive to the recognition of cultural differences as complementary rather than contradictory or compartmental. The remainder of this book is devoted to exploring how this works. That requires, first of all, a tool kit of concepts suited for discussing automation and its cultural impact.

The Modes and Evolution of Information Management

The basic process we will be studying is *information management*. It requires two things: there must be information to manage, and there must be a way of managing it. I am using "information" in the colloquial sense to refer to the stuff of knowledge: facts, circumstances, ideas, concepts, and so on. We do not create information totally anew every time we think about it, nor does it utterly disappear when we are not thinking about it. Therefore this knowledge must be stored somewhere. Any repository for storing information may be termed *memory*. To manage information is to do something with or about it, that is, to process it. This includes procedures for storing information in memory, retrieving it from memory, and organizing, analyzing, and otherwise using or applying it in various ways. Information processing is carried out by *intelligence*.

Many kinds of beings have memory and process intelligence, including animals and plants. Here we are interested in just two kinds of memory and intelligence. *Human memory* holds information in human minds, while *artificial memory* refers to other repositories that store information. These include handwritten and printed texts, graphic images, and electronic databases.[5] Symmetrically, *human intelligence* refers to information processing that is conducted by human beings, while *artificial intelligence* is the province of mechanical information processing devices. Preeminent among these today, of course, are computers.

These distinctions between types of memory and intelligence may be deployed to distinguish three kinds or modes of information management. In the *oral mode*, information stored in human memory is processed by human intelligence.[6] In the *textual mode*, human intelligence processes information stored in artificial memory. And in the *automated mode*, artificial intelligence processes information stored in artificial memory.

All three modes are fully active today, they regularly work in combination with each other, and probably the bulk of information management is still conducted in the oral mode. Nevertheless, there is an evolutionary or a historical aspect to them. The oral mode has existed for as long as we have been human. For by far the greatest part of the history of our species, extending well into the twentieth century for nonliterate societies, it stood virtually alone. Using human intelligence to process information stored in human memory, individuals combined their different knowledges and skills for getting food, finding shelter, defending themselves, entertaining themselves, creating art, understanding the world, defining their relationship to the supernatural, and so on. In the process, they settled the entire globe and developed the astounding richness and diversity that characterize human cultures. Some limited artificial memory existed in the form of bodily adornments, rock drawings, and other artworks, but it is difficult to imagine the existence of any artificial intelligence at all during that long period.

The textual mode became a significant factor only about 2,500 years ago, when alphabetic writing was invented, and it received a major boost some 550 years ago with the introduction of printing with moveable type. The great leap in artificial memory was not necessarily matched by a decline in human memory. Indeed, training human memory probably grew even more rigorous as people strove to memorize large bodies of written material (Yates 1966). But the hallmark of the textual mode is a massive expansion of storage space in artificial memory. Written records greatly facilitated trade and bureaucratic administration and were therefore pivotal in the accumulation of wealth and the rise of cities and states. Writing also stimulated the development of philosophy, science, and scholarship of all descriptions. Records stored in human memory tend to change as they are transmitted through the generations, while those stored in writing are fixed. Thus perusal of old documents demonstrates more clearly than consulting human memory how conditions in the past differed from those of the present. This stimulates curiosity about exactly what the changes are and why they occurred, or, in other words, an increased interest in history.

The automated mode of information management was inaugurated when artificial intelligence emerged with devices such as the abacus and the Jacquard loom, a technique invented by Joseph-Marie Jacquard in 1801 to produce intricate weaving designs mechanically by controlling the action of the loom with patterns of holes punched in pasteboard cards. Because I am defining artificial intelligence broadly as mechanical information processing of any sort, I include as further steps the invention of the telegraph in 1844, as well as subsequent inventions of the telephone, radio, and television. The automated mode has received a massive boost in the last few decades with the widespread use of computers. This has transformed and expedited global communication and the management of large quantities of information to such a degree that even people like myself, who lived large portions of their lives in times before computers became ubiquitous, wonder how we ever got along without them.

It is clear from this historical sketch that as the textual and automated modes have been added to information management, the node of growth or progress has been concentrated in the artificial sector. The capacities of individual human memory and intelligence have not materially increased in at least the last 3,000 years, and probably much longer. That is, people today do not have memories more capacious than Homer's, or powers of reasoning more trenchant than Socrates'. By contrast, in that same period, artificial memory and intelligence have expanded phenomenally. The reason is that human intelligence and memory are governed by the glacial Darwinian principles of biological evolution, while their artificial counterparts develop by the much more rapid process of cultural evolution, where, in Lamarckian fashion, each generation learns and builds upon the accomplishments ("acquired characteristics") of its predecessors.

Human beings, of course, are responsible for this entire evolutionary process. However, of the total amount of available information, the proportion stored in artificial memory is far larger today than it was a few centuries or even a few decades ago. Artificial intelligence is now superior to human intelligence in certain kinds of information processing, such as rapidly searching large bodies of data for specific items, mathematical calculation, and the solution of complex problems governed by multiple rules (Baldi 2001:92–93). Future advances in artificial intelligence will doubtless enable it to rival or surpass human intelligence in other areas as well. But this does not mean, as some anticipate, that human beings are in jeopardy of being replaced by computers. On the contrary, the strongest points of human and artificial intelligence are very different, and they complement each other. Much information processing today is carried out jointly by both forms, and the participation of artificial intelligence creates new opportunities for the application and growth of human intelligence. Thus even as automation plays a larger role in thinking, and precisely because of it, the scope and power of human intelligence expand as well. The following chapters aim to demonstrate how the confluence of the automated mode of information management with the oral and textual modes alleviates the trouble with culture, opening it by replacing its categories and preordained certainties with more flexible, contingent, and complementary ways of thinking.

Chapter 4

The Human Rage to Classify

When I was in high school in the mid-1950s, I wrote a paper on the religion of the Maya. My procedure was to go to an encyclopedia and read the entry on the Maya. Then I read a few of the books recommended by the encyclopedia article that seemed most pertinent to my topic. Finally, I made an outline organizing the material I wanted to use in a way that seemed coherent, conjured up a few general conclusions, and wrote the paper accordingly.

A high school student doing a project on the same topic today would proceed quite differently. The first step would probably be to find relevant Web sites using an Internet search engine. The student would read through the material in several of those sites, extract what seems most relevant and interesting, and assemble it in the final product. That product might be a traditional paper, or it might take another form such as a PowerPoint presentation or a Web site. To get a more immediate sense of how people today would address the project, I searched the Internet search engine Google for "Maya religion." It returned 10,100 sites, of which I consulted the first twenty. These included two photo essays, a general site on ancient Mesoamerica, an online catalog to accompany a museum exhibition, an entry in a site devoted to world religions, an online encyclopedia article, two brief essays written by three boys, ages eleven and twelve, information about the Fifth European Maya Conference, two sites showing the place of the Maya in classifications of Internet sites, a list-serv discussion about similarities between Maya religion and Christianity, and six sites consisting of college class projects.

What struck me most about the difference between the information sources I used nearly fifty years ago and those that would be used today is that mine manifested much more internal organization. The encyclopedia article and the books to which it referred me were all carefully crafted texts presented in an ordered manner and designed to be read from start to finish. Taken as an aggregate, the Web sites turned up by Google had no organization at all, sharing only the fact that they dealt in one way or another with Maya religion. Taken individually, some of them were organized internally in the same way as the sources I used in high school, notably the Internet encyclopedia article and one of the college projects, which took the form of a traditional term paper. The others were different. Especially interesting were the other class projects and the museum catalog. These took the common Web site form of a home page and then several other pages dealing with various aspects of the topic: pantheon of gods, rituals, calendar, sociocultural context, and so on. The constituent pages did not build on each other as successive parts of an article or chapters in a book often do. Instead, each was largely self-contained, and they could be read in any order. Hyperlinks sprinkled throughout enabled the reader to jump instantly between the pages of the site and sometimes to other Web sites entirely. None of them had much in the way of general conclusions tying all of the information together. The stand-alone quality of the pages, the absence of conclusions, and the hyperlinked invitations in midtext to go elsewhere all indicate that such a Web site is less—or, at the very least, differently—organized than a printed text. If the printed text marshals carefully selected evidence to reach particular conclusions, the Web site form of presentation invites the user to consider an array of relatively diverse facts and interpretations, not all that closely connected to each other and not necessarily pointing to any overall conclusions at all.

People tend to suppose that the world really is organized as their socially established information structures say it is. Therefore, a different way of organizing information brings with it a different way of viewing the world. Classification dominates the presentation of information in the pre-automated context. The articles, books, compendia, and catalogs that convey information about plants, animals, and other aspects of the natural world, the scholarly disciplines, the types of political and philosophical systems, the collections in museums and libraries, and so on are always already organized in prepackaged classifications. Information presented in terms of classificatory schemes channels people to view the world and to act in terms of the received categories of those schemes. To the degree that such cultural categories are clear, unequivocal, and uncritically embraced, and to the degree that they designate key concepts and fundamental values, their adherents will be threatened by or impervious to the different categories of other cultures, regarding them as contradictory or irrelevant to their own. This generates hostility or indifference between societies with different cultures and within culturally diverse societies, and thus is part of what I have been calling the trouble with culture.

On the other hand, information secured and presented by automated technologies is less strictly organized and often not classified at all. This loosens the grip of culture, allowing a more open-minded attitude toward unfamiliar facts and ideas. Hence, the possibility of mutual understanding, harmonious relations, constructive engagement, and cooperation within and between societies increases, and that constitutes a step toward alleviating the trouble with culture. This chapter and the next will discuss what classification is and probe its controlling effect on worldview. Subsequent chapters will address how automation bypasses classification and therefore simulates more fluid, liberal ways of thinking.

CLASSIFYING

The information processor in the oral and textual modes of information management is human intelligence. A preeminent characteristic of human intelligence is that it organizes the diverse items of information it encounters according to some kind of classification. Probably this is because the human mind seeks to simplify the great multiplicity of things and events of the world, and it does so by lumping them together in a manageable number of related categories. Underlying all classificatory schemes are the assumptions that things come in distinct categories, that those categories are relatively fixed as to the sort of things they include and exclude, that the categories have certain relationships to each other, and that an important aspect of knowledge consists of knowing what things belong to what categories and what the relations between the categories are. All of this provides people with confidence that the world they inhabit has a stable form, and that the things and events found in it are ordered, meaningful, and, to one degree or another, predictable.

However, the sheer fact that many different systems of classification exist indicates that while it may be natural for human intelligence to classify, there is nothing about either human intelligence or external reality that requires that the classification be done in any particular way. Classificatory schemes are products of culture. But, of course, that is the statement of an anthropological analyst. The great majority of people do not think of the classificatory schemes that they live by as cultural constructions. Having no experience with anything else, they assume that they encapsulate the independently existing, intrinsic organization of reality. As foundational to many other concepts and convictions, classificatory schemes are one of the most basic ways that culture impresses itself on its adherents.

The cultural variability of classification struck me while doing anthropological fieldwork on Rapa, the southernmost island of the Austral archipelago, in French Polynesia.[1] What particularly impressed me was, compared with ourselves, how little emphasis Rapans place on time in ordering the events of their daily lives, and how much on space.[2] Many of them had only the vaguest notion of their own age, much less of that of people close to them. Nor did temporal sequence seem very meaningful to them. One woman told me, for example, that she was about forty years old, and she imagined that her first child must be around twenty-five and her third about thirty. Rapans do recognize three distinct stages of life, which can be roughly translated as childhood, youth, and adulthood. But those terms refer more to lifestyle and state of mind than to age brackets, so certain "youths" are chronologically younger than some "children," and others are older than some "adults."

If Rapans appear to Western eyes as being unattuned to matters pertaining to time, then they are remarkably acute with reference to space. Indeed, they seemed to be preoccupied with location. Where people are or have been or are going was a topic of consuming interest. Common forms of greeting were "Where are you going?" or "Where are you coming from?" When people related their activities of the day to extended family members at supper in the cookhouse, they would invariably specify where they had been, where they saw other people, and the location of all noteworthy events. Similarly, a striking feature of Rapan myths and legends is the careful specification of the location of all events in the story. I gained the distinct impression that by exchanging this information, Rapans mentally classified the jumble of events surrounding them according to *where* they occurred. The categories in their scheme of classification corresponded not to sequential points along a stream to time but to named tracts of land on their island.[3]

This, of course, is just one of many ways of classifying. Of the numerous kinds of classificatory schemes that exist, I propose to discuss just two: classifying by correspondence and classifying by taxonomy. I have chosen these two because they seem to be the most widespread forms of classification, they are quite different from each other, and their differences reveal important insights into the logic of classification.

CLASSIFICATION BY CORRESPONDENCE

As described in the well-known book *Black Elk Speaks*, the Sioux classify a variety of qualities according to the four cardinal directions, the sky, and the earth. West, for example, is associated with the color black, rain, and warfare; east with red, plenty, and peace; south with yellow, growth, and the unity of the nation, and so on (Neihardt 1972:22–24). This kind of classification, based on correspondences, is quite different from the taxonomic form that is more familiar to Western readers. The distinctive feature of taxonomy is hierarchy, whereby general categories are divided into subcategories at any number of levels. Correspondence, on the other hand, divides many different kinds of things (plants, animals, human groups, gods, days, seasons, and so on) into the same number of categories and then maps them on each other. Items sharing the same position are thought to have something in common.

The Hopi have a system similar to the Sioux. Each direction is linked to the color of the anthropomorphic deity who is thought to sit there. These are further associated with types of plants, animals, and other natural phenomena in an elaborate set of correspondences. The associations of "Below" (see Table 4.1) are multiple, because the deity who sits there is many colored and the source of all life (Hieb 1979:578).

The Chinese system, as described in the *Nei Ching* (*The Yellow Emperor's Classic of Internal Medicine*) (Veith 1966), is a correspondence scheme based on the number five. The five directions are the cardinal points of the compass plus the center. Corresponding to the directions are fivefold divisions of many different phenomena: the internal organs or viscera, external body parts, seasons of the year ("long summer," or what in the United States is called "Indian summer," brings the number of seasons to five), the elements, and flavors.

TABLE 4.1
Hopi Correspondences

Direction:	Northwest	Southwest	Southeast	Northeast	Above	Below
Color:	Yellow	Green	Red	White	Black	Grey, or All Colors
Flower:	Mariposa Lily	Blue Larkspur	Indian Paintbrush	Evening Primrose	Sunflower	Many Flowers
Cultivated Plant:	Corn	Bean	Squash	Cotton	Water-melon	Many Plants
Type of Corn:	Yellow Corn	Blue Corn	Red Corn	White Corn	Black Corn	Sweet Corn
Predatory Animal:	Mountain Lion	Black Bear	Red Wolf	Bobcat	Golden Eagle	Badger
Game Animal:	Deer	Mountain Sheep	Antelope	Elk	Jackrabbit	Cottontail

Source: Adapted from http://www.daphne.palomar.edu/ais100/hdirect.htm (accessed October 25, 2002).

In the interest of simplicity, Figure 4.1 omits many phenomena that also belong to the system, such as emotions, musical tones, colors, animals, the planets, and still others (Veith 1966:21).

The system defines several kinds of relationships among items. Those classified at the same position are connected to each other. This is important, among other things, for medical diagnosis, for the health of internal organs can be determined by examining the external body parts located at the same position in the classification. Thus healthy muscles and nails signify a flourishing liver, the condition of the lips indicates the health of the spleen, and so on. The rationale behind this is often quite concrete. The vital essence of food, for example, is thought to go from the stomach to the liver, and from there to the muscles and nails (p. 196). Therefore, unhealthy muscles and nails signify that the liver is not functioning properly.

The five positions also are arranged in a particular sequence, indicated by the solid arrows on the diagram. This cycle, without beginning or end, is an elaboration of the eternal oscillation between dominant yin (the passive principle, associated with north, winter, water, etc.) and dominant yang (the active principle, associated with south, summer, fire, etc.). In this sequence, items located at one position are thought to produce their counterparts at the next. This is immediately obvious in the succession of

FIGURE 4.1
Chinese Correspondences

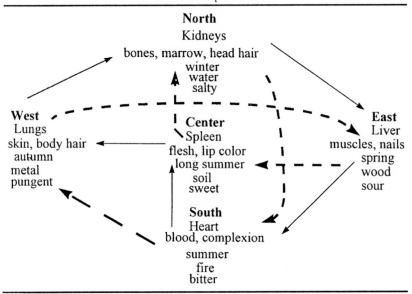

the seasons. The five elements, which are probably the foundation upon which the entire fivefold structure is built (Veith 1966:19), also produce each other according to this sequence: water produces wood, wood produces fire, fire produces soil, soil produces metal, and metal produces water. The rationale for these relationships for the most part is self-evident (ashes from fire become soil, metal ore is obtained from soil), except perhaps the production of water from metal. This may refer to the condensation that appears on cold metal in humid weather.

If one sequence among the five positions pertains to production, then another connotes subjugation. This cycle is indicated by the dotted arrows on the diagram. Again, the five elements exemplify this relationship most clearly: water subjugates fire (by extinguishing it), fire subjugates metal (by melting it), metal subjugates wood (by cutting it), wood subjugates soil (by piercing and turning it, as with a digging stick or wooden spade), and soil subjugates water (by damming it) (Veith 1966:19). One way these subjugative relations relate to health is through the flavors. Excessive saltiness hardens the pulse (signifying a blood disorder), too much sweetness causes the bones to ache and the hair of the head to fall out, and so on around the cycle (p. 141).

Although we have barely scratched the surface, the main characteristics of the Chinese system are clear. One of them is that, as with the Sioux and Hopi schemes, the particular items are fixed in their positions. Thus wood, spring, and the lungs are always together. The complexity of the Chinese scheme stems from the kinds of relations that are posited between items at a single position and, even more, between items in different positions. Other correspondence systems achieve complexity by associating items in different combinations. Aristotle followed this principle when he derived the four elements from different combinations of the two sets of opposed categories—hot and cold, wet and dry. Thus fire is hot and dry, air is hot and wet, earth is cold and dry, and water is cold and wet. This conception of the elements and their qualities prevailed in the West throughout the Middle Ages.

Astrology parlays the combinations and permutations characteristic of this kind of classification by correspondence into a system of immense complexity. It combines Aristotle's four elements with three "decans." The decans control activity, "cardinal" being associated with direct action, "fixed" with persistence and determination, and "mutable" with richness of experience. For their parts, the elements control temperament: earth produces practicality; air, intellect; fire, leadership; and water, emotion (Barton 1994:42; McIntosh 1969:9, 12; Graubard 1953:56; Sakoian and Acker 1973:10–19). The twelve possible combinations of the four elements with the three decans are associated with the signs of the zodiac (see Table 4.2). Thus leadership by direct action is associated with Aries, leadership by persistence with Leo, and so forth.

The signs of the zodiac are named for constellations of stars in segments of the sky associated with each month (McIntosh 1969:7). The earth's surface too is divided into twelve segments, called houses of the horoscope. These combine space and time, defined by points on the horizon calculated by positions of the sun at two-hour intervals as the earth rotates on its axis. The houses of the horoscope correspond to the signs of the zodiac, the first house (rising sun) being associated with Aries, the tenth house (midheaven) with Capricorn, and so on (Sakoian and Acker 1973:7).

Casting a horoscope is ultimately an act of classification, for it amounts to situating an individual at a particular confluence of influences determined by the twelve signs of the zodiac, the twelve houses of the horoscope, and other factors. That process, as with the system of astrology in general, has been greatly simplified in this brief description. Perhaps enough has been said, however, to recognize astrology as yet another kind

TABLE 4.2
Signs of the Tropical Zodiac

Sign	Element	Decan
Aries	Fire	Cardinal
Taurus	Earth	Fixed
Gemini	Air	Mutable
Cancer	Water	Cardinal
Leo	Fire	Fixed
Virgo	Earth	Mutable
Libra	Air	Cardinal
Scorpio	Water	Fixed
Sagittarius	Fire	Mutable
Capricorn	Earth	Cardinal
Aquarius	Air	Fixed
Pisces	Water	Mutable

Source: Adapted from McIntosh 1969:128–32 and Sakoian and Acker 1973:33–52.

of classification by correspondence.[4] Such classifications represent immensely complex and powerful organizations of information that have occupied generations of scholars in the task of understanding and applying their intricacies.

TAXONOMIC CLASSIFICATION

The other major kind of classification is taxonomic. It is widely used to classify plants and animals, the scholarly disciplines, languages, books in libraries, recipes in cookbooks, sites on the World Wide Web, and a great deal more. As with classification by correspondence, taxonomies organize things, qualities, and other phenomena in a meaningful cosmos by identifying relationships between them. But a very different kind of relationship is now in play. The hallmark of taxonomy is hierarchy. The typical form of a taxonomic classification is the inverted tree, with the trunk or most general category at the top and its various branches or more specific categories ramifying below at any number of levels until the concrete items being classified are reached (Richmond 1965:5).

Taxonomic classification is found in cultures all over the world. So general is it that some authors have claimed it to be a universal feature of human classifications of plants and animals, reflecting affinities that naturally exist among those phenomena (Hunn 1975a:320, 1975b:19; Berlin 1992:xi). But Roy Ellen argues, to my mind persuasively, that classifications are culturally conditioned, because they stem less from individual perceptions than from collective matters such as historical contingencies, linguistic structures, metaphorical extensions, and ritual prohibitions (Ellen 1993:149–50).[5] In the West, for example, taxonomy is based on the following constellation of assumptions: (1) nature is an ordered system, (2) that system can be known and described, (3) natural phenomena are comprised of essences that take the hierarchical form of genera and species, and (4) therefore, the proper representation of those essences should also be hierarchical, or taxonomic (Slaughter 1982:3–4). For much of Western history a further assumption was that because nature's order is God given, a goal of scientific taxonomy is to reveal God's plan for the world (p. 7). Slaughter lends historical support to Ellen's contention that taxonomic classification schemes are products of cultural and historical conditions by noting the fact that while all of these propositions enjoyed wide acceptance in the West in the seventeenth century, later many of them lost much of their force (pp. 4–5).

The concept of taxonomic classification raises a number of problems and challenges peculiar to it. An ideal of any taxonomy is that there should be one and only one place for everything it classifies. In reality, however, things are seldom so clear-cut. Some seventeenth-century scholars were convinced that the fault lay with the imperfections of natural languages. To rectify the problem, Bishop Wilkins, René Descartes, Gottfried Wilhelm Leibniz, and others set out to create a new, "philosophical language," the words of which would reflect the intrinsic nature of things and their classificatory relationships. In the language concocted by George Dalgarno, for example, garlic and onions rejoiced, respectively, in the names *nebghnagbana* and *nebghnagmuba* (Slaughter 1982:150).

While ordinary language unquestionably does introduce ambiguities, the subject matter itself often resists falling neatly into the taxonomic categories regardless how precisely they are defined (Jonker 1964:55–63). Lewis Henry Morgan's classification of societal types was based on the presence of elements of material culture, such as fire, bow and arrow, pottery, agriculture, metallurgy, and so on. He placed Polynesian societies in middle savagery because they lacked the bow and arrow (Morgan

1877:10–11).[6] However, Polynesians also could have been classified as middle barbarians, because they did have pottery and domesticated plants and animals. Again, in the subject classification that George Watson Cole devised for picture postcards, "windmills" appears twice: once in category 10,c, under "Ferries and Canals," and again in category 38,c, under "Architecture, fine" (Cole 1935). As the items to be classified are more multifaceted, the impossibility of definitively classifying them in only one category becomes starkly obvious. Consider the classification of library books. To be sure, a book must occupy a single place on the shelves, and catalogers determine that by assigning it a single call number based on what they consider its most important subject matter. But few books treat one and only one thing, and this is explicitly recognized by classifying them under several other topics in the subject catalog.

Any taxonomy is based on criteria that are used to determine where particular items should be placed. Those who hold that taxonomic classification reflects natural affinities and differences among phenomena assume that the criteria they use are embedded in the nature of things. But it is difficult to square this with the fact that different criteria are in fact used in different schemes, resulting in different placements. In his zoological classification, Aristotle relied mainly on morphological criteria, because, he imagined, that captures animal essence (Slaughter 1982:32). But in the classifications of French taxonomist de Moulin and the Rangi people of Tanzania, animals are organized by habitat, according to whether they frequent the air, land, or water (Slaughter 1982:31; Kesby 1979). Again, classifying human societies in terms of levels of sociopolitical organization (as bands, tribes, chiefdoms, and states) results in a different array than Morgan's technologically based scheme or a classification that uses religion (e.g., animism, polytheism, monotheism) as its criterion.

This poses the question as to whether any classificatory scheme can reflect the essence of reality. If the cake can be cut in different ways, then which is the right one? Diderot, one of the leading lights in the ambitious eighteenth-century project to summarize all knowledge in a great encyclopedia, recognized that because classification schemes are hatched from human presuppositions, none of them could aspire to capture reality as a thing in itself. In his eponymous article "Encyclopedia," he wrote: "The universe . . . has an infinite number of aspects by which it may be represented, and the number of possible systems of human knowledge is as large as the number of these points of view. The only system from which arbitrariness would be excluded is . . . the one that existed from all eternity in the mind of God" (quoted in Joy 1991:128–29). For his part, Diderot did not share the sanguine expectations of many others, that the classifications they were devising did in fact recapitulate the one God had in mind.

Of the innumerable applications of taxonomic classification, I wish to discuss in greater detail just two: the scholarly disciplines and materials in libraries.

Taxonomies of Branches of Knowledge

Certainly every society encompasses a set of skills and a body of knowledge too great for any individual to master. Therefore, people specialize. Perhaps the most elaborate system of specialization in existence is the scholarly disciplines in Western culture. In the sixth century B.C., the Greeks considered knowledge mathematics. Pythagoras divided it into what later became known in Latin as the quadrivium, or conjunction of four roads: arithmetic, music, geometry, and astronomy. These all pertained to the external world, and the basis of their conjunction was that they were all based on numbers. Later, Aristotle added three more roads pertaining to the inner world of mind—grammar, rhetoric, and logic—which became the Latin trivium. In what may be thought of as an early conceptualization of the sciences and the humanities, together the quadrivium and trivium constituted the seven liberal arts (Park 1847:28–29, John Younger, personal communication). This is a classic form of taxonomic classification, knowledge being divided into two major divisions, one with four subdivisions and the other with three. Further elaborations were then made. In the sixth century A.D., for example, Senator Cassiodorus divided the discourse produced by rhetoric into two types of positions or cases: rational and legal. At the next level he distinguished among five types of legal and four types of rational cases, and these are further subdivided at yet another level (Cassiodorus 1946: 148–53).

Classification of the arts and sciences was a major preoccupation in Europe and America from antiquity through the nineteenth century, and a great many different taxonomies were proposed.[7] The following brief descriptions of just a few are intended to convey a sense of their variety and the different criteria underlying them. In the second century A.D.,

Galen theorized that intellectual functions originated in the brain, which was composed of three ventricles. Nemesius Emesenus, in the fourth century, associated the ventricles with the three faculties of mind: imagination at the front of the brain, reason in the middle, and memory at the back.[8] This view, widely held until the late seventeenth century, was the basis of the influential classification of the arts and sciences devised by Francis Bacon in 1605 (Olivieri 1991:66–71). He attributed natural and human history to memory. Imagination produces poesy or "feigned history," so called because, unlike natural and human history, it is not constrained by truth. Reason is the source of philosophy, which Bacon defined broadly as the study of deity, humanity and laws of the material world, physics, and metaphysics, the latter including mathematics (Bacon 1605; Park 1847:29).

Bacon's Spanish contemporary, Juan Huarte, also used the three mental faculties as the basis for his classification, but he came up with sharply different results. For example, while imagination gets rather short shrift in Bacon's scheme, Huarte saw it as a broad category encompassing all of those arts and sciences that deal with harmony, proportion, and figure. This includes "poetry, eloquence, music, preaching; practice of medicine; mathematics and astrology; the government of a republic; military art; painting, drawing, reading; becoming a courteous, acute, polite, refined man; being able to invent and build new pieces of machinery; and finally, being able simultaneously to dictate to four different secretaries, in an orderly and systematic way, scholarly material from four different fields" (Olivieri 1991:72).[9]

By the nineteenth century, people had left off classifying the scholarly disciplines according to the faculties of the mind or brain and organized them instead in terms of their subject matter. This brought the division of the disciplines in line with the taxonomic classification of things in the world, with each category of things having its own discipline dedicated to its study. An interesting example, which also embodies the goal of philosophical language to make the names of the disciplines indicative of their place in the classificatory scheme, was proposed in 1816 by American Augustus Woodward. He developed a taxonomy of the fields of knowledge that adhered to a set of nine "laws" that he devised for good classification (Woodward 1816:240–48). These included such sound advice as comprehensiveness, correctness, not classifying the same thing in more than one place, and, when it is necessary to coin new terms for certain disciplines, using words that are unambiguous and easy to remember, having "strength, and grace, and ease, and euphony" (p. 247). To avoid ambiguity, his names for the individual sciences end in "-ia," and those for higher levels in "-ica." Woodward dubs the highest level of all, the entire universe of knowledge, "catholepistemia" ("catholepistemica" would be more consistent with his rule). Catholepistemia has three "provinces": knowledge relating to matter (Hylica), to mind (Ennoeica), and to matter in union with mind (Hylennoeica). Hylica is divided into two "classes," Hylennoeica into three, and Ennoeica has just one class, for a total of six classes. The classes are further divided into eighteen "orders," which are again divided into a total of sixty-four sciences.

Thus geometria, goniametria, and ancylometria are the sciences in the order geometrica, which together with the order arithmetica will form the class mathematica. This is the class in the province Hylica that deals with abstractions about matter. The other class in that province, Physica, has several divisions that concern aspects of matter in its own right. The province Ennoeica, dealing with mind, has only one class but three orders. These are Psychica (mind possessed in a material vehicle, divided into the sciences of animal and human psychology), Pneumatica (mind of spiritual beings such as angels and God), and Eusebica (the relationship between human mind and divine mind), divided into four sciences devoted to the study of heathen, Jewish, and Christian religions and to philosophical thinking on the subject of religion.[10] The reader can judge the extent to which Woodward adhered to his law of devising terms that are euphonious, graceful, and easy to remember. In any case, he is a prime representative of the taxonomic mentality that seeks to classify everything in one and only one place, together with a terminology that precisely matches the classification.

Auguste Comte, prime proponent of French positivism, developed a classification of the sciences also based on subject matter that was simpler and enjoyed wider currency than Woodward's. Standing prior to all of the sciences in Comte's scheme is mathematics, which provides the most general and abstract tools for work in any of them. The sciences themselves fall into two main categories: inorganic and organic. The inorganic sciences consist of astronomy, physics, and chemistry. These each have subdivisions; for physics, they are barology (study of gravity), thermology (study of heat), acoustics, optics, and electrology. The organic sciences consist of physiology and social physics or sociology (it was Comte who originally coined that term). Sociology is not divided further, but physiology splits at the next level into the studies of: (1) the structure and composition of living bodies, (2) the classification of living bodies, (3) vegetable physiology, (4) animal physiology, and (5) intellectual and affective physiology (psychology) (Comte 1830:16–17).

In addition to its hierarchical structure of categories and subcategories, Comte's scheme had a linear quality to it, because he organized the sciences in a logical order (which also corresponded fairly well with their historical development). The arrangement is such "that the rational study of each category [science] be founded on knowledge of the principle laws of the preceding category, and becomes the basis for the study of the following one" (Comte 1830:71, my translation). This is grounded in the assumption that new law-governed properties emerge at each step as one passes from astronomy to sociology. A mouse, for example, obeys the laws of physics (if you drop it out of a window, it will fall) as well as chemical combinations. But when considered physiologically, the mouse is subject to certain new laws not operative in physics or chemistry, such as those governing respiration, alimentation, and reproduction.

Although he devised an important classification of the sciences, Comte feared that an unintended consequence of such classifications is that people would focus on the differences between the sciences and consider each as independent field of study. He insisted that all science is a single, unified enterprise, and that any divisions among them were meant only to help resolve the complex problems they face (1830:36). The logical connections he drew among the sciences testify to that conviction, but the history of specialization demonstrates that his concerns were justified. Taxonomic classification is conducive not only to specialization but to the inward-turning, isolating form of specialization that we have called compartmentalization.

The various disciplines are examples of what Stanley Fish (1980:14) in a larger context has called "interpretive communities": relatively enduring groups of people marked by a tendency to think about the same things in the same way. That is an entirely understandable and effective way to proceed as knowledge accumulates beyond the capacity of any individual to control it all, but the cost is limited communication between disciplines. As an interpretive community, each discipline defines the work to be done within it on the basis of a set of assumptions. These assumptions become axiomatic, so that any questioning of them within the framework of the discipline is not encouraged (Toulmin 1982:234, 256). The disciplines become similar to distinct societies with different cultures. Clifford Geertz has even said that they should be studied ethnographically, as anthropologists study cultural differences, to enable translation between them (Geertz 1983:155–56). That notion is embedded in the title of Tony Becher's book, *Academic Tribes and Territories: Intellectual Inquiry and the Culture of Disciplines* (1989).

Disciplinary insularity flows from the logic of taxonomic classification. Taxonomies carve up reality into distinct categories, and each category becomes a "field" to be cultivated by a particular discipline. Education and research in a discipline include discriminating between what does and does not belong in its field, and therefore, between what one need and need not learn, what one need and need not investigate. This tendency has been sharply criticized by environmentalists, proponents of holistic medicine, and many others for ignoring important connections between things that are not closely related taxonomically. At its worst, immersion in this mentality leads scholars to dismiss research that extends beyond the disciplinary boundaries by sniffing disdainfully: "but that's not anthropology" (or psychology, or biology, or whatever). Even at its best, it operates on the assumption that certain subject matters naturally belong together, while others are remote and less pertinent. This keeps people ignorant of findings in other disciplines that may be relevant and important to their work. Philosophers who would analyze the springs of human action conjure up intricate, fictitious "thought experiments" from their own minds rather than attending to accounts of actual behavior from historians and social scientists. Experimental psychologists concentrate exclusively on what transpires in the laboratory without reference to the social context of their observations as elucidated by sociologists, anthropologists, or even social psychologists.

The separation of the disciplines also has a political aspect. What Michel Foucault said about the regulation inherent in disciplinary organization pertains also to the academic disciplines: "Discipline fixes; it arrests or regulates movements; it clears up confusion. . . . Hence, the fact that the disciplines use procedures of partitioning and verticality; that they introduce, between the different elements at the same level, as solid separations as possible" (Foucault 1977:219–20). Speaking more specifically of the academic disciplines, Cary Nelson and Dilip Gaonkar (1996:2) talk about "the unwritten and unsigned pact post World War II disciplines made with state power. It was a McCarthy-era pact guaranteeing silence and irrelevance from the humanities and collaboration from the social sciences, a pact disguised by (and structured in terms of) the proprieties of disciplinarity and its proper boundaries, limits, and conduct." In seeking to maintain the canon of Great Books and the disciplinary division of academic labor, conservative organizations such as the National Association of Scholars and individuals such as Allan Bloom and Harold Bloom are on the side of perpetuating that pact. In striving to achieve equal status for writings by minority and Third World authors and incorporating interdisciplinary approaches in their work, scholars from women's studies, Native American studies, cultural studies, and similar orientations seek to break the pact by bringing capitalism and state power under critical scrutiny (see Nelson and Gaonkar 1996:2; Appadurai 1996:34; Grossberg 1996; Rooney 1990).

Disciplinary specialization perpetuates itself through education. Courses are labeled by discipline, and curricula are designed to "cover" that discipline. To major in a subject is to be trained in the basic findings, methods, and theories associated with it. So, for instance, college students begin with Introduction to Sociology, and majors then take a variety of upper-division courses in various facets of the discipline, such as Urban Sociology, Sociology of Deviance, and Sociological Theory and Method. In this system, the way students master a skill or expand knowledge is dutifully to assimilate information that has been filtered and vetted by disciplinary conventions, and then they go on to apply it and perhaps teach it to others. "Disciplines police their boundaries," write Nelson and Gaonkar (1996:3), "by training their members to internalize them, naturalize them, and then fancy themselves free as birds." Contrary to the popular opinion that education liberates the mind, this form of "subject-oriented learning" accomplishes precisely the opposite by organizing and conditioning students' thinking in accordance with the preestablished classificatory categories set down by the disciplines (Cranton 1994: 10–19). In this way, education brings the other common meaning of the term discipline into play: it disciplines learners; it becomes a means of exercising Foucault's (1977) disciplinary power over them. If people are to avoid being dominated by disciplinary knowledge, then in mastering a discipline they must be vigilant against being mastered by it (Usher, Bryant, and Johnston 1997:83, 89).

Taxonomies of Records of Knowledge

Before writing, virtually all information was managed in the oral mode, and human memory was the storehouse for the vast majority of records of knowledge. Written records became the preeminent form of artificial memory in the textual mode of information management, and especially with the invention of printing, artificial memory held an increasingly large proportion of records. Artificial memory has several advantages over human memory. For one, records can be stored in the memory of any human being only for the lifetime of that individual. Hence, they must be periodically transferred from one person to another. In this process the records are susceptible to change through forgetting on the part of the older person, faulty memorization on the part of the younger one, and abbreviation or embellishment on the part of either or both. As long as they are not intentionally or accidentally altered or destroyed, records stored with proper care in writing, printed text, or electronic media last indefinitely without change. Again, there is a limit to the amount of information a single human memory can store. The sum total of information in any culture exceeds that limit by storing parts of it in different minds. But then, in order for someone else to access certain information, it is necessary to discover who knows it and to find those persons. In contrast, there is theoretically no limit to the amount of information that can be stored in a single repository of artificial memory, whether a library[11] or a collection of databases such as the Internet.

The introduction of artificial memory did indeed usher in an increase in the amount of available information, and it has been growing ever since. Among many others before and after him, in 1847, the Rev. Roswell Park raised the alarm that the sheer mass of recorded information was getting out of hand. As evidence for the disturbing state of affairs, he listed the holdings of several of the world's libraries in the mid-nineteenth century. The largest of them—the Bibliothèque du Roi in Paris—held 700,000 volumes. Harvard University had 50,000, and the Library of Congress had 25,000. His best estimate was that the total number of different printed works in existence was some 2 million (Park 1847:25).

If that was enough to worry Rev. Park, imagine his reaction to some corresponding figures today. According to the Association of Research Libraries, Harvard now holds some 14.4 million volumes. My own institution, the University of Kansas, which did not even exist when Rev. Park was writing, holds 3.7 million volumes—almost double what Park estimated for the whole world in his time.[12] Considering further that a great deal of material is now stored in media other than print—microforms, tapes, DVDs, CD-ROMs, computer mainframes—it is obvious that the amount of recorded information continues to multiply astonishingly and is likely to continue to do so into the indefinite future.

It has long been clear that it is impossible to control the growing number of records stored in artificial memory without organizing them in some way. Current responses to the problem, utilizing automation, will be considered in later chapters. Textual mode solutions take the form of cataloging documents; that is, sorting them in accordance with some classificatory scheme. Numerous such schemes have been devised, and their workings reveal further interesting applications of and variations on the classificatory worldview.

Relatively little is known about which cataloging systems may have been used in the great ancient libraries of Ashurbanipal or at Alexandria and Pergamum. Greeks of the third century B.C. organized works according to a few very general subjects and name of author. The number of lines was recorded, and the first few words of a work were more important than the title. These might be alphabetized, but never beyond the first letter (Strout 1969:6–7). (First-line indexes are still used for poems and hymns.) Although one might imagine that catalogs would have been very useful in Roman times, we have "not one fragment of them or even one reference to their existence" (p. 9).

The earliest classification of records for which detailed information exists is from China. Although the Chinese classification discussed earlier—linking the elements, seasons of the year, organs of the body, and so on—is based on correspondence, the catalog of the imperial library devised by Liu Xiang in 6 B.C. was taxonomic. His scheme was known as the *Seven Summaries*. "The Confucian scriptures stood apart at the head of the system; other distinct categories then followed—schools of philosophy; poetic literature; certain specialized fields of knowledge—military science, divination, medical techniques; each class then subdivided into sections to make, for its original purposes, a well articulated system" (Dudbridge 2000:4–5, see also Drège 1991:95–102, who dates this development at 26 B.C. rather than Dudbridge's 6 B.C.). By the seventh century, the seven summaries had evolved into a system with four main divisions—Confucian scriptures, histories, masters, and literary collections—each with its subdivisions. This remained the main classification of library holdings in China to the end of the nineteenth century and for ancient works down to the present (Drège 1991:120, 137; Dudbridge 2000:6).

In early Europe, most libraries were located in monasteries. They seldom held more than a few hundred volumes. No one thought to classify them, and their catalogs were little more than inventories of holdings. By the tenth through the twelfth centuries, collections were growing, some monasteries having as many as 600 or 700 volumes. If anything, however, lists of manuscripts contained even less information than they had in the ninth century. If there was any subject classification at all, in most cases it was limited to two categories: "biblical" and "humanistic" (Strout 1969:9–11). The richest catalog I have encountered from medieval times is the library of the Friars of York. Its holdings were organized according to several subjects, including bibles, bible commentary, canon law, civil law, medicine, mathematics, and philosophy (Humphreys 1990:xvi).

For the most part, however, catalogs did not evolve from simple inventories of holdings into subject classifications to help store and find books until the beginning of the eighteenth century (Strout 1969:20). Initially, the various libraries devised their own classification schemes. The first unified system dates from 1791, when the French revolutionary government sent cataloging instructions to libraries throughout the country. The card catalog was born at the same time. For reasons having more to do with wartime shortages of materials than any advantage perceived in using a card form, the instructions proposed that cataloging information be recorded on playing cards. They even recommended that aces and deuces be used for the longest titles, presumably because they had the greatest amount of empty space (pp. 20–21).

Drège (1991:89–90) points out that bibliographic classifications are descended from classifications of the arts and sciences. This is anything but surprising, for the fact that written documents are produced by people working in one or another of the fields of human endeavor makes it natural to classify those documents according to the same fields. So the scheme that Thomas Jefferson devised to catalog his personal library (which was the kernel of the Library of Congress) was based on Bacon's classification of knowledge according to the three mental faculties. Jefferson organized his books under the general headings of history (corresponding to the faculty of memory), philosophy (reason), and fine arts (imagination), further broken down into a total of forty-four "chapters" (Park 1847:30–31; Gilreath and Wilson 1989).

Jefferson may have classified his books according to subject, but where they stood on the shelves was another matter. His library in Monticello held smaller books on the top shelves, medium-size ones on middle shelves, and the largest ones at the bottom. Books were shelved according to size, with books of like size and belonging to the same chapter of the subject catalog shelved together. Each book was labeled with its own call number, consisting of the number of the chapter in which it was classified and its acquisition number within that chapter (Gilreath and Wilson 1989:7–8).

Because books often deal with several subjects, they are ill suited to the classifier's dream of placing everything unequivocally in one and only one place. Catalogers do attempt to identify a book's primary topic, which they use for assigning it a unique call number and place on the shelves. But it is also listed under any number of topics in the subject catalog. Curiously, the idea that a book not be limited to a single subject category did not occur to anyone until the 1820s, and it was a long time before it gained general acceptance. When the British House of Commons debated the value of classified catalogs and indexes in the 1830s, one of the arguments against it was that someone sufficiently interested in a topic could just consult an author list because he certainly knew everyone who had written on his topic anyway (Strout 1969:21–22).

When Melville Dewey was an undergraduate library assistant at Amherst College in the early 1870s, call numbers were locating devices that specified the library room and shelf position where books were kept. This practice necessitated time-consuming call number changes whenever books were moved from one place to another or, worse, when the entire collection was transferred to a new library building. The tidy-minded Dewey moved to rectify the situation by designing a cataloging system with call numbers that remained the same no matter where books might be shelved in a particular library (Rider 1969:285–86). At least as important, the scheme itself represented a taxonomic classification of all knowledge. It was divided at the first level into ten large categories: (0) generalities, (1) philosophy and psychology, (2) religion, (3) social sciences, (4) language, (5) natural sciences and mathematics, (6) technology (applied sciences), (7) the arts, (8) literature and rhetoric, and (9) geography and history. Each of these was divided into several levels of subcategories, with the ultimate result that every work was assigned a unique number that indicated its position in the conceptual scheme and also served as a call number designating its proper location on the library shelves. The Dewey Decimal System, originally published in 1876, was the most detailed, rational, and complete library cataloging scheme to have been devised until that time, and its core principles informed all subsequent library classification systems. It continues to be used by most public libraries in the United States and in many other countries as well.

THE CONTRASTING LOGICS OF CORRESPONDENCE AND TAXONOMY

Classifications of every sort share the fundamental property of establishing meaningful relations among things, transforming the otherwise chaotic universe into an organized system. But correspondence and taxonomic classifications achieve that of quite different logics of relationship. The difference is captured by the distinction that semioticians have drawn between metaphor and metonymy, or paradigm and syntagm, or, in the more ordinary terminology introduced long ago by Hume, between resemblance and contiguity. Resemblance is based on similarities between things. Resemblance in its various degrees is the basis for lumping canoes and rowboats together and distinguishing them from sailboats, as well as for classing canoes, rowboats, and sailboats together in contrast with automobiles and airplanes, for grouping women together and distinguishing them from men, for taking human beings as one kind of thing distinguishable from animals, and so on. Contiguity, on the other hand, relates different things on the basis of their commonly being found together. The relationships between bread and butter, canoes and lakes, or wealth and power are based on contiguity.

Taxonomic classification is based on resemblance. Dogs and wolves are lumped together and distinguished from domestic cats and jaguars on the basis of resemblance. On a higher level, resemblance also determines the classing of all of those together as mammals and distinguishing them from reptiles. Degree of resemblance is the governing criterion all up and down the taxonomic ladder. Systems of classification by correspondence, on the other hand, are governed by contiguity. The co-occurrence of different items may be fixed, as when north, kidneys, and water are constantly conjoined in the Chinese system. Or, it may be variable, as in astrology or Aristotle's system, where the possible combinations of hot and cold with wet and dry produce the four elements: earth is cold and dry, water is cold and wet, and so on. Still, whether the association is fixed or permuted, the basis of relationship is contiguity.

Because of this difference in the logics of relationship, the general types of worldview associated with the two forms of classification differ in several ways. One is that classification by correspondence is conducive to predicting the future. If events of a certain kind are associated with a particular conjunction of days, planets, or other circumstances, then events of that kind may be expected every time that conjunction occurs. Hence, there is great interest among astrologers and in other communities that classify by correspondence to calculate when such conjunctions will occur so that future events may be foretold. The logic of taxonomic classification provides no comparable ground for prediction.

Another difference is that taxonomy traffics more in abstraction. Mary Slaughter argues that taxonomic classification is associated with writing, and she maintains further that things described in writing tend to be decontextualized from concrete reality. This disposes people to think about those things in analytic, abstract ways (Slaughter 1982:38–48, see especially p. 40). Many anthropologists who have studied classification systems would question any necessary link between taxonomy and writing, pointing out that taxonomic classification is also widespread in preliterate societies. But Slaughter's conclusion—that taxonomy is associated with abstract thinking—is nevertheless perceptive and useful. Concrete things are found only at the lowest level of taxonomic classifications. All of the higher levels—"primates" and "mammals," "Romance languages" and "Indo-European languages"—are increasingly general abstractions that represent groupings of concrete items. Therefore, people who view the world taxonomically are accustomed to think in terms of abstract, general categories. Classification by correspondence produces generalizations, if that is even the appropriate term for them, of a very different sort. It does stipulate general categories consisting of items that belong together: red corn, red wolf, and antelope for the Hopi, liver, wood, and sour for the Chinese, and so forth. But unlike taxonomy, the members of these categories are concrete.[13] Correspondence schemes do not identify abstract properties for such groupings in their own right, nor do they group the groupings together into still larger ones.

The predilection to abstraction makes taxonomic classification an ideal battlefield for the debate between realists and nominalists. This question, which has vexed thinkers in the West since Plato and Aristotle, has to do with whether only concrete particulars exist (the nominalist position), or whether general categories also exist in their own right (the realist position) (Lovejoy 1964:227–30; Slaughter 1982:21–22). It is entirely understandable that people who think every day in terms of the general categories characteristic of taxonomic classifications would wonder about the reality of those categories. That question is less likely to come up in the context of classifications by correspondence, where abstractions are less prevalent.

One of my main theses is that culture exercises a divisive influence in large, internally diverse societies. Classification, as a prime representative of culture, is implicated in this, but in somewhat different ways depending on the kind of classification involved. Correspondence and taxonomy are similar in that both can produce contradictory or compartmental differences between groups with different cultures. Where they differ is that taxonomy is considerably more likely to generate compartmental differences between groups with the same culture. That is, taxonomy is more prone to specialization. Given its logic of resemblance, taxonomies group or separate things depending on the degree of similarity between them. From that perspective the most instructive things to know about something are to be found among its siblings and immediate antecedents and descendents on the taxonomic tree, for they are most likely to have something in common with it. One can learn more about dogs by comparing them to wolves than to leopards, or bacteria, or water. Connections between things such as bodily organs and seasons of the year are so remote in the taxonomic way of thinking that it is nonsense to mention them in the same breath. It is not surprising that as knowledge accumulated taxonomically oriented Western scholars would immerse themselves in one narrow field and lack the time or inclination to study the rest. Specialization can quite easily lead to isolation and compartmentalization.

In classifications by correspondence, on the other hand, things that are classed together because they are understood to co-occur are often disparate from a taxonomic point of view, such as golden eagles, the color black, jackrabbits, and watermelon for the Hopi. Even when the complex division of labor produces full-time specialists, it is difficult in correspondence systems to produce the level of compartmental specialization that emerges with taxonomic classification. In a correspondence system such as astrology, for example, where the signs of the zodiac result from each of the four elements combining with each of the three decans in different circumstances and with different outcomes, it would be nonsense to specialize in one element, or one decan, or one combination, while ignoring the rest. Again, the systematic associations among diverse entities not only within but also between the five major categories in the classification scheme underlying traditional Chinese medicine require the physician who would diagnose and treat a patient for, say, disease of the liver, to take into account a wide variety of influencing factors, including (to name only a few) the condition of the muscles and nails, the season of the year, the flavors in the food the patient eats, and the patient's emotions. It is unlikely that a Chinese physician would be the target of the charge so often leveled against highly specialized Western doctors: that they focus exclusively on the disorder and are oblivious to the general condition of the patient.

Chapter 5

Classification and the Common Law

The preceding chapter argued that classificatory schemes impress a certain view of the world on their adherents. People tend to assume that the categories of their classification are given in the nature of things, that one can locate everything that is already known about any topic by consulting the category of information pertinent to that topic, and that when new knowledge is acquired, an important task is to decide to which category it properly belongs. To people with presuppositions such as these, the world has a fundamentally determinate and permanent form, and the correct ways of thinking about it and behaving in it are fairly clearly laid down. This leads to the rigidities of thought that I have associated with the trouble with culture. This brief chapter, a case study of the common law, aims to give a more concrete picture of the classificatory mind-set and its consequences.[1]

LEGAL INFORMATION

Recorded information is simultaneously the necessary food and a potential poison for a system of common law. The toxic element comes from sheer volume. Common law rests on the principle of *stare decisis:* that cases should be decided in the same way as similar cases have been decided in the past. This has caused the alarm to be repeatedly raised that the accumulation of case records over time imposes an intolerable burden on practitioners. If they all are considered potential precedent for deciding new cases, then the sheer mass of recorded information grows beyond the capacity of any attorney or judge to control, and the edifice of common law threatens to collapse under its own weight.

The inception of the problem can be traced to the late twelfth century, when the courts began to recognize written records. Prior to that time English law operated exclusively in the oral mode of information management. Evidence consisted of what witnesses could recollect, and litigants were required to provide proof of claims only for the period covered by "living memory." This was the outermost limit—about a century—of the memory of the oldest living person. Everything before that was known as "time out of mind," and beyond consideration in court proceedings.

English law entered the textual mode in 1194, when written "plea rolls" began to be kept as a record of what had been transacted in court (Grossman 1994:5).[2] By 1235, writing had become important enough to court proceedings that "a plea was judged to be void because no written document had been produced" (Goody 1986:161). This period can be regarded as marking "the formal beginning of the era of artificial memory" in English law (Clanchy 1993:152). Written records, of course, are not subject to the cutoff point of living memory. They remain consultable for as long as they are kept. Hence, the threat of legal literature growing beyond the limits of manageability began with the keeping of written records and has grown with the increasing volume of those records.

"COMMON-PLACING"

The problem was how to bring some sort of order to the accumulating mass of legal information. A popular means for doing this in the sixteenth century and beyond was to keep "common-place" books. Essentially these were notebooks designed for taking reading notes in an organized fashion. They contained headings under which students and professionals would record important information that they had read. At first "common-placing" was considered primarily a means of jogging memory, and the headings were idiosyncratically chosen, but by the seventeenth century, they were becoming standardized. In the early nineteenth century, law teacher David Hoffman, of Baltimore, recommended that students and professionals keep separate notebooks on eight general topics, among them Exceptions to General Principles; Leading Cases; Obiter Dicta and

Remarkable Sayings of Distinguished Judges and Lawyers; and Remarkable Cases Modified, Doubted, or Denied. Each notebook was to be alphabetically arranged according to several subtopics and filled with information that the owner gleaned from ongoing reading. Standardization of topics developed to the point that in the nineteenth century common-place books were even published with the headings already printed in them, followed by blank pages for the user to enter notes (Hoeflich 2001).

The significance of common-placing extends well beyond convenience. Michael Hoeflich (2001) suggests that common-place headings came to serve as templates in terms of which lawyers organized their studies, and, therefore, their thinking. This nurtured a consensus about what the law is. Thus the legal profession and the law itself are grounded not only in a certain body of information but also and perhaps even more importantly in particular ways of organizing and accessing that information. Hoeflich's analysis is an example of one of the primary theses underlying this entire work: that how information is organized and accessed influences what that information means and how people view the world.

SUPPLY-SIDE CONTROL VERSUS AN "APPALLING GLUT"

For a while common-placing eased the burden of coping with centuries of accumulating case law recorded in artificial memory, but it certainly did not erase it. A supply-side strategy is to restrict the growth of the literature. This approach has been adopted primarily by the British. They tried to prevent publication of redundant cases with the explicit intent of keeping the body of case law available as precedent within manageable limits. The goal was to limit cases that may be used as precedent to the relatively few that modify a principle of law, enunciate a new principle, settle a doubtful question, or are in some other way particularly instructive.

The American tendency, on the contrary, has been to publish many cases. Its onerous consequences soon became apparent. A committee of New York lawyers formed in 1873 noted that in the seventy-nine years since 1794, some 590 volumes of law reports had been published in the United States. That amounted to more than half the total of English law report volumes that had been published in a period of 565 years, from 1307. The phenomenal volume of American reports was due less to a principled intention to arm lawyers with a rich field for potential precedent than to the ambition to make some money. The New York committee said that publishers, finding the legal profession willing to buy whatever they would print, published as much as they could (Grossman 1994:59).[3]

As it happened, one private publisher managed to gain quasi-official status as the place of record for American case law. This was the West Publishing Company of St. Paul, Minnesota. Finding that his publication of Minnesota opinions was not sufficiently profitable, in 1879 founder John West combined them with opinions from five surrounding states to form a series of volumes called the *North Western Reporter*. Over the next eight years, West added new sets of volumes covering federal opinions and opinions from the rest of the states, divided into six additional regions. The resulting totality came to be known as the *National Reporter System*. West's volumes became necessary holdings for law schools and law firms throughout the country (Grossman 1994:81–83).[4] According to one assessment, "This privately held, secretive publisher of court decisions has become, literally, the sum and substance of American jurisprudence" (p. 81).

Although West did eliminate many rival publishers, that did not ease the situation that constitutes the thread of our story: the increasing difficulty to manage legal information as the case record grows over time. Indeed, by its profit-driven policy of publishing as many appellate decisions as possible, West materially exacerbated the problem. As Grant Gilmore wrote: "The West Publishing Company, whose interest in jurisprudential theory I assume to have been minimal, . . . made a contribution to our legal history which, in its importance, may have dwarfed the contributions of Langdell, Holmes, and all the learned professors on all the great law faculties. After ten or fifteen years of life with the National Reporter System, the American legal profession found itself in a situation of unprecedented difficulty. There were simply too many cases, and each year added its frightening harvest to the appalling glut. A precedent-based, largely non-statutory system could not long continue to operate under such pressures" (Gilmore 1977:59).

KEY NUMBERS

Attorneys were not without devices to help them wade through the flood. These included distillations of important principles and preeminent precedent in the form of treatises, encyclopedias, and *Restatements*.[5]

Another came from the West Publishing Company itself. Introduced in 1896, it is known as the American Digest System or, more familiarly, the key number system. It is relevant to this analysis as an outstanding example of how a classificatory scheme acts as a comprehensive and powerful tool for organizing and finding information, and how that has important consequences for the way users of the scheme act and think. Basically, it works in the following way. Building on a taxonomic scheme originally devised by brothers Austin and Benjamin Vaughn Abbott for the *New York Digest* in 1860, West divided the law into seven major categories. These were further divided into more than 400 topics, which are divided again, in as many as four hierarchical levels, into a total of over 40,000 subtopics. Subtopics under each of the 400-plus topics are assigned "key numbers." West editors carefully analyze each opinion they publish and classify the points of law addressed in it according to topic and key number. For example, homicide is one of the 400-plus topics. It is divided into eleven subtopics, one of which is "Murder." Murder, in its turn, is further divided into eighteen categories, and one of those is "Persons Liable." This is assigned key number 29. Thus any reference in a judicial opinion to persons liable for murder is classified under "Homicide 29."

A *Digest* appears at the end of each volume of cases (or "reporter") that West publishes annually for each region. This is an index listing all cases in the volume according to West's 400-plus topics, arranged alphabetically, and key numbers. By looking up key number 29 under Homicide in the *Digest*, an attorney can identify all of the cases in the volume that discuss persons liable for murder. Cumulative digests for all West reporters also were published at ten-year intervals until 1976, and thereafter, due to the increased number of cases, at five-year intervals. As these are extremely large, West also publishes smaller cumulative digests limited to federal cases, to the particular regions within the National Reporter System, and to most of the individual states. Cumulative digests are used in exactly the same way as the digest at the end of a single volume. By consulting topics and key numbers in cumulative digests, one can find opinions pertaining to any point of law as discussed in cases from any jurisdiction and from any time from the seventeenth century to the present.[6] Coming at a time when the volume of legal information stored in artificial memory threatened to exceed the capacity of researchers to access it, "the systematization involved in the West key-number system may be largely responsible for rendering the common law manageable enough to survive in the United States" (Grossman 1994:79; see also Berring 1987:25).

IMPLICATIONS

I have already noted that people assume that their classificatory schemes reflect the actual organization of reality. This is another way of articulating Marshall McLuhan's powerful idea that the medium is the message: techniques for managing information about the world became assumptions about the nature of the world. In the present case, the categories of the taxonomic schemes for classifying legal information have been reified into principles thought to exist in their own right. The key number system in particular, Robert Berring argues, ascended to prominence far above mere case retrieval. "[It] provided a paradigm for thinking about the law itself. Lawyers began to think according to the West categories" (Berring 1986:33; see also Bintliff 1996:343).[7] As Hoeflich suggested for common-placing centuries ago, Berring sees the West categories as defining what the law is for recent generations of lawyers.

The standing of those categories has been bolstered by the structure of legal education. The basic first-year law school curriculum, introduced in the latter nineteenth century at Harvard by Dean Christopher Columbus Langdell and taken up by virtually all American law schools, was designed according to the same basic categories of law that inform the West digests.[8] Having been immersed in these categories both in their training and in their ongoing legal research, lawyers took what were actually organizing decisions of Langdell and the West Publishing Company to be the intrinsic structure of the law (Berring 1994:22–23; Bast and Pyle 2001:287). That they are, instead, only one way of organizing a particular body of legal information—that associated with American common law—is evident from the fact that lawyers in Louisiana, with its civil law system, are often frustrated by the distortions that result from West's efforts to classify their cases according to its key numbers.[9]

Any classificatory system that establishes relatively independent categories invites specialization in one or another of them, and we have argued that taxonomic classifying is particularly prone to the isolating kind of difference that I have called compartmental. This has been evident in the legal profession. Lawyers specialize in criminal law, family law, contracts, insurance, and so on. Moreover, the law as a whole has held itself as a field of endeavor separate and distinct from all others, and did so largely because its practitioners thought that it was grounded in a unique and an esoteric body of information.

The law has its own literature, such as case records, legal encyclopedias, and law reviews. These form something of a closed system, in that lawyers seldom consult literature beyond them, and people from other disciplines rarely consult legal literature. In addition to being insulated from the outside, legal literature has a unique internal hierarchical organization into primary, secondary, and tertiary sources. Primary sources are the law itself. They consist of constitutions, statutes, and judicial opinions in case law, of which the decisions of higher-level appellate courts carry the most authority. Secondary sources are commentaries on the law: treatises, encyclopedias, textbooks, monographs, and law journal articles. Finally, tertiary sources are tools such as the West key number system, devoted to locating pertinent primary and secondary legal sources. The hierarchy is visible in citation practices. Judicial opinions, as primary sources, most commonly cite other judicial opinions. While they also may cite secondary sources, those carry less weight. It is virtually unheard of for a primary source to cite a tertiary source. Secondary sources such as treatises and law review articles heavily cite primary sources, but they also freely cite other secondary sources. Secondary sources cite tertiary sources only rarely, and then primarily as instruction for how to use them . . . although, as the present discussion illustrates, a secondary source literature is growing around the proposition that tertiary sources have an important influence on the organization of the law and the modes of legal thinking. The point to be stressed here is that everything remains within the confines of the law. As Charles Collier put it, "A central implication of Langdell's case method was that, in the study of law, one need not venture beyond appellate judicial opinions" (1991:200).

Another basis of the law's isolation from the rest of society is its parochial regime of training. Traditionally, law schools have tended to keep aloof from other schools in the university—they usually have their own buildings. The law library is separate from other university libraries and contains little other than legal literature, a situation that promotes informational distance between the law and other bodies of knowledge (Katsh 1995:68). The segregation of students has been nearly total. Undergraduate programs in law are rare. Law courses are peopled nearly exclusively by law students, who in turn take nothing outside of the law school. In my own institution at least, law courses are listed in a separate timetable, and the law school even follows a different academic calendar from the rest of the university. Little wonder that lawyers, immersed for three years in this separate world, go forth in the conviction that the law is a domain unto itself.

Conclusion

My general argument is that classification, as a primary means for the expression of culture, is conducive to the contradictory and compartmental differences that I have linked to the trouble with culture. More specifically, taxonomic classification of information is especially prone to compartmental difference. It fosters a view of reality as divided into distinct segments, with communication and interaction being more frequent within the segments than between them. This chapter has demonstrated that the law, with its self-contained and hierarchically organized body of information, exemplifies this in several ways. The segmental organization of reality is visible first in the distinction between law and other professions and parts of society, and again in the notion that the several categories of law distinguished in law school curricula and in devices such as the key number system reflect the intrinsic structure of the law as something that exists in its own right. Compartmental difference between segments is most clearly represented by the isolation of law schools from other parts of universities, the tendency for cases to be argued and decided exclusively within the context of the body of legal information, and the maintenance of legal reasoning and practice as an esoteric activity understood only by those within the profession. Michael Hoeflich and Jasonne O'Brien contend that the law as a profession began in the twelfth century with the development of a body of specialized knowledge, canonical texts, and modes of access to them (forthcoming). As with other professions, its persistence is related to the maintenance of those methods and materials in esoteric form. Thus within the larger society, the law has guarded a domain of private knowledge available only to those who belong to the profession, speak its specialized language, and know its peculiar procedures. Outsiders who run afoul of the law or stand in need of its ministrations must be represented by attorneys and frequently have only the barest understanding of what is happening in negotiations or in court. If one stops to think about it, this is most curious. Complex commercial transactions aside, the law, after all, is intended to regulate the relations of people with each other. Surely if people know anything, they should know the rules governing how they should get along.

This discussion has been limited to the time when the management of legal information was conducted exclusively in the oral and textual modes. More recently the law has opened noticeably, due in part to the automated mode of information management, which has revolutionized legal research during the last quarter century. The consequences of that revolution are highly pertinent to my basic argument. This other, newer side of the law will be considered in some detail in chapter 8, after the advent of automation and the shift from classification to indexing have been introduced in a more general way.

Chapter 6

Automated Classification and Indexing

Some years ago I wanted to use, as the epigraph for a chapter I was writing on vocational interest testing, the following passage from Mark Twain: "A round man cannot be expected to fit a square hole right away. He must have time to modify his shape." I was quite sure that the passage occurred in Twain's book *Following the Equator*, but I needed to verify it. I went to the library and pulled the thick volume off the shelf. It had no index, so I began scanning each page. After nearly an hour of eye-breaking tedium, I finally found it. Had the full text of that book been available in electronic form, I could have conducted a keyword search with my word processor for, say, "round man," and I would have found the passage in a matter of seconds.[1] Essentially what I was doing by scanning the pages, and also what I would have been doing in the keyword search, was constructing an index for the book. A funny kind of index perhaps, having but a single entry, but an index nonetheless.

The point of this little story is that when it comes to indexing, artificial intelligence has certain advantages over human intelligence. But there is an equally important counterpoint: artificial intelligence is inferior to human intelligence, for purposes of classifying. The following pages explore this point and counterpoint with the objective of establishing the more general point that our growing reliance on an automated means of accessing information has brought about an increase in indexing and a corresponding decrease in classifying. The still-larger claim is that this shift has an array of important, if rarely recognized, implications. To

83

prefigure them in synoptic fashion, I maintained in chapter 4 that classification is a primary means of perpetuating the fixed categories of culture.
That helps keep culture closed and thus feeds the divisive problems that I
have called the trouble with culture. In this and subsequent chapters, I
argue that indexing, as a means of accessing information different from
classification, is not (or, at least, not as much) governed by culture. Indexing thus liberates thinking from the established categories of culture. This
entails a greater likelihood that differences will be recognized as complementary rather than contradictory or compartmental, and that represents
an important step toward more open culture, more independent and creative thought. Indexing is therefore an antidote to the trouble with culture. Moreover, it does all of this in a way that is more grounded in
habitual behavior, and therefore more effective, than the frontal assaults
on closed culture mounted by cultural relativism and postmodernism, discussed in chapter 3. To embark on this line of reasoning, we need to begin
with a clear idea of the difference between classifying and indexing, and
why the latter fits more comfortably with the automated mode of information management.

CLASSIFYING AND INDEXING

The crucial difference between classifying and indexing lies in how they
organize information, particularly the relation between parts and wholes.
Indexing stresses the parts. It is an analytic procedure that divides information into particles and treats them independently. Thus a typical index
is a finding device that connects a symbol (usually in the form of a word)
for a particular topic to whatever material is pertinent to that topic in a
body of information stored in human memory, in print, or electronically.
Using the index of a book enables one to retrieve information about a certain topic from widely separated places in the book. In the same way, a
keyword search locates information on a topic from many documents in
an electronic database (see Bolter 1991:22).

Classifying, on the other hand, emphasizes wholes. Discussed at
length already, it is a synthetic procedure that combines and organizes bits
of information according to some meaningful scheme.[2] The body of information may be as small as the contents of a single article or as large as the
entire corpus of recorded knowledge. The classification scheme involved
may be as unique and focused as the table of contents of one book or as

general and widespread as the Dewey Decimal or Library of Congress systems for cataloging all materials in libraries. In all cases, the distinctive feature of classifying is that it sorts particular items into the categories of a general scheme, thus applying ideas about how items relate to each other in the context of a meaningful whole.

In the oral and textual modes of information management, the distinction between classifying and indexing is not sharply drawn, because human intelligence, the information processor in both of those modes, handles both functions comfortably. Indeed, in the oral mode, the two can hardly be distinguished. Consider the "art of memory." The only storage place for information in the oral mode is human memory, so great emphasis is placed on training it. In the West, such training was long considered a special scholarly activity, included within the seven liberal arts as part of rhetoric (Yates 1966:5, 50). Aquinas, following Aristotle, specified two rules for cultivating memory. First, things to be remembered should be put in good order, and second, they should be associated with similitudes or images that are concrete and easy to recall (pp. 34, 85–87). Remembering things in this way is variously called mnemotechnics, mental indexing, or the art of memory (Yates 1966:2–4; Clanchy 1993:179). Images of buildings with their various rooms and furnishings were often used for this purpose. A body of information would be mentally connected to a certain building, and categories or particular facts within that body of information would be memorized in association with the various rooms in the building or objects in each room. Then, thinking of the object or room jogged one's memory to deliver the corresponding unit of information. When it was important to recall the information in a particular order, one would mentally visit the places in a certain sequence (Yates 1966:2–3, 295; Ong 1958:119; Clanchy 1993:173–78). Is the association of information with the rooms and objects in the building a case of classifying or indexing? The distinction seems to make little difference.

It also is blurred in the print indexes of the textual mode of information management, for they often incorporate one degree or another of classification. Pulling a book randomly from the shelf in front of me, Anthony Standen's *Insect Invaders*, I see the following entries in the index:

Plum curculio, 86, 182
Potato beetle, 13, 137–38, 192
Praying mantis, 187
Predators, 185–88, 190–95

Prickly pear, 97–201
Propolis, 105–06
Prussic acid, 166–67, 168

Taken individually, each of these entries is an example of pure index-ing: a single topic with no identified connection to any other topic. Two topics in the index, however, take a different form. One of them is:

Pest control, by quarantine, 144–50; by chemicals, 153–70; other meth-ods of, 172–201; eradication and, 205–23.

The other is "Insects." It has twenty-two divisions, including "classes of," "bodies of," "forest," "imported," "harmful to man and animals," and "good." These two entries are internally organized as general topics divided into categories. They represent a hybrid approach called, not sur-prisingly, classified indexing. The same can be said of much more complex classification schemes such as the Dewey Decimal System, with its divi-sion of all knowledge into ten great categories, each of which has several levels of subcategories. A common use of the Dewey subject catalog is to locate books in a library. When used in that way, the Dewey system oper-ates as a classified index: a classification scheme that also serves the func-tion of a finding device.

A sliding, overlapping relation between classification and indexing also may be glimpsed in the history of encyclopedias. The encyclopedic movement began in the late eighteenth century with the lofty goal of pro-viding a systematic compilation of all knowledge. With the accent on "sys-tematic," early encyclopedias were primarily classifications of knowledge in coherent, hierarchical schemes. In the twentieth century, however, encyclopedias began to concentrate on presenting easily accessible infor-mation on a large variety of particular topics, arranged in alphabetical order (Dolby 1979:167–68). As they did, their primary function shifted from classification to indexing.

If classification and indexing often elide in the textual mode of infor-mation management, then the distinction between them is pronounced in the automated mode, where the information processor is artificial intelli-gence. The reason is that artificial intelligence is very good at the one and very poor at the other. Automated keyword searching is an outstanding example of pure indexing. Using the form of intelligent activity that Hubert Dreyfus (1992:291–93) calls "associationistic," it matches the word or phrase of a query with material contained in a database. When it comes to indexing, artificial intelligence is far superior to human intelligence. It is fast: contemporary search engines consult millions of documents in less than a second. It is general: most printed documents lack indexes, but *any* digitalized text or database is subject to keyword searching. And it is customized: users select the keywords that are most appropriate for their needs rather than being bound by choices made by authors, cataloguers, or indexers.

Good as it may be at indexing, artificial intelligence is very bad at classifying. This is partly because artificial intelligence has great difficulty recognizing metaphors, ironies, synonyms, homonyms, and levels of generalization that human intelligence uses so regularly and so effortlessly as it engages in classifying. More precisely, classifying belongs to the fundamentally different kind of intelligent activity that Dreyfus calls "nonformal" (p. 293). It cannot be reduced to matching lists or employing strict rules or algorithms. "Pattern recognition in this domain is based on recognition of the generic, or of the typical, by means of a paradigm case. Problems on this level are open-structured, requiring a determination of what is relevant and insight into which operations are essential, before the problem can be attacked. Techniques on this level are usually taught by generalizing from examples and are followed intuitively without appeal to rules" (p. 294). Operating in this way, different classifiers will often reach different conclusions depending on how they weigh and combine many different criteria. Consider, for example, the ongoing debates between "splitters" and "lumpers" as to whether fossil finds should be classified as a new species or as belonging to an already recognized species. Dreyfus argues that nonformal activities such as this cannot be reproduced by artificial intelligence.

The power of automation as an indexing tool and its weakness as a classifier account for why, in the automated mode of information management, the prominence of indexing increases and that of classification declines.

How Automated Indexing Works

When computers were first coming into common use, automated systems engineers found it impracticable to design information retrieval on the basis of subject classification or any other method except free text retrieval of words, commonly known as keyword searching (Bintliff 1996:346–47). When it comes to text management, what artificial intelligence does exceptionally well is find matches. Especially when combined with Boolean operators (AND, OR, NOT) and proximity controls (instructions that the keywords must not be separated by more than a specified number of words), keyword searching becomes a powerful tool for locating occurrences of particular words or combinations of words in one or more documents. That is, it indexes the documents for those words or word combinations.

Automated indexing works differently depending on the kind of search program used and the number of documents to be searched. The simplest is the "find" function of a word processor such as WordPerfect or Microsoft Word, which is limited to searching single documents. The user enters a string of characters (part of a word, a single word, a sequence of words, numbers), and the word processor scans through the document to locate matches with the search string. These are presented one at a time, in the order they appear in the document, it being necessary to click the "find next" button to move from one match to another. Less than exact matches can be found with "wildcards." "?" represents any single character, so a search for "th?s" will return both "this" and "thus." "*" is used for any combination of several characters, so a search for "th*s" produces "otherwise" and "the purpose," among many others. Microsoft Word also has a "sounds like" option for searching. It seems, however, only to return results with the same initial sound. Thus a search for "thing" produces "think" but not "bring," while a search for "bring" in the same document produces "brings" and "Berring" but not "thing."

Indexing multiple documents is more complicated. Especially interesting are Internet search engines. These have the daunting task of indexing the staggeringly numerous and utterly unorganized sites on the World Wide Web according to users' search queries (Maze, Moxley, and Smith 1997:16–17). A typical way to accomplish that is by discovery programs called by various terms such as robots, crawlers, or spiders. These are programs that locate Web sites. They accomplish this by visiting all of the hyperlinks found in one site, all of the hyperlinks in each of the linked sites, and so on through an indefinite number of generations of links until millions of sites have been located. The discovery robot alphabetizes the addresses (URLs) of the sites it has found and eliminates duplicates. A harvester robot then visits each of those sites and develops a list of the words (except "stop words" such as "an," "the," "of," and so on) appearing in it. A few search engines, such as Altavista, include all of the nonstop words in each site, but most limit their lists in one way or another, such as to title, abstract, or the first 100 words in the site. For each word on the list, the harvester robot also records information about how many times it appears in the site, where it appears (in the main title, a subheading, the general text), and so on. A database consisting of a master list of words is created, with each Web site entered under each word found in it. When someone enters a query in a search engine, the words in the query are compared to those in the database. The results of the search are all of the Web sites that have been listed under the words in the database that match the words in the search query (Maze, Moxley, and Smith 1997:14–26, 96; Kustron 1997).

While a simple listing of the occurrences of a keyword in order of appearance may be adequate for searching single texts, sheer bulk renders this insufficient when it comes to searching the Internet. It was estimated that in 2000, there were about a billion Web pages in existence, and that their number was doubling every three to six months, with some 600 new ones being added every minute (Arnold and Colson 2000:44). On May 24, 2002, the search engine Google claimed to search 2,073,418,204 Web pages, a number that doubled to 4,285,199,774 as of July 17, 2004, and nearly doubled again to 8,168,684,336 by August 30, 2005. In the face of magnitudes this large, it is clear that even the special powers of artificial intelligence are hard pressed to keep pace. In 2000, the robots of most search engines managed to visit and analyze only about a third of all Web sites (Belew 2000:296). The number of sites located with most search terms is staggering; it is not uncommon for a search engine to return hundreds of thousands of sites that satisfy the query. The user can diminish the results by refining the search query, but search engines themselves also cope with massive numbers of finds by automatically evaluating their relevance to the search query and presenting them in rank order. This represents another advance that artificial intelligence achieves in indexing. Manual indexing only lists places where certain topics are addressed; usually it does not specify which one of those places contains the richest information on the topic.

Still, the way search engines achieve their ranking is related to how human beings use print indexes. Searching for a topic in the index of a book, one is likely to go first to places where several successive pages are indexed for it, because an extended discussion of the topic is more likely to satisfy the user's need than just a mere mention. Or, looking in an index to periodical literature, one is likely to go first to those periodicals that have many articles on the subject rather than just one or two, because publications in periodicals with a particular interest in a topic probably contain the most important articles on it. Similarly, search engines rank sites automatically by frequency and location of keywords. That is, the more often terms in the search query occur in a site, and the more they occur in strategic places (the title, section headings), the higher the ranking of that site (Kustron 1997). Another automatic method, used by Direct Hit, is to rank sites on the basis of the number of visits they receive. A third, pioneered by Google, ranks sites on the basis of the number of other sites to which they are linked, taking into account the rank of those other sites on the basis of sites that link to *them*, and so on (Arnold and Colson 2000:44; Jacso 1999).

CAN ARTIFICIAL INTELLIGENCE CLASSIFY?

For all of their ingenious ranking methods, search engines still return findings as a disorganized list that includes many documents irrelevant to what the user is looking for, and that may not include the most relevant ones. This problem might be solved, as one dream has it, if artificial intelligence could be programmed to classify as human intelligence does. The result would be an optimal system of information storage and retrieval in the automated mode of information management that combines the computer's capacity to conduct rapid searches with the librarian's ability to organize it.[3]

I do not think this is likely to happen because, as I have said, artificial intelligence is not very good at classifying. This may appear to fly in the face of the facts, because subject classifications are prominently displayed and available for use in online library catalogs, Internet search engines, and other automated systems. This is entirely true, but they do not really automate classification. The subject function of an online library catalog simply provides automated access to classifications that have been produced by human catalogers in accordance with the Library of Congress or Dewey Decimal classification systems. The Web sites retrieved through the classification systems offered by search engines such as Yahoo!, the Open Directory Project, and many others also have been selected and categorized by human rather than artificial intelligence.

To develop a truly automated classification of, say, the World Wide Web would be highly desirable, because it is unrealistic to imagine that human classifiers could control the entire and growing avalanche of information on all topics available there. And the effort clearly has been and is being made—although, as the following review will demonstrate, with very limited success. At this point we enter into an area of technical research and development in artificial intelligence. I will try to touch on some of the high points, although much current work will be left aside and surely some new schemes will have been introduced by the time what I am writing now reaches print. It is important to remember that the concern here is not with the technical aspects of cutting-edge research projects but with the cultural consequences of information technology. Hence, the focus is on the main features of programs in general use.

Nearly all projects to automate classification have tried to make artificial intelligence mimic human intelligence, the ultimate objective being computer decisions that are indistinguishable from those made by human beings. Human classification consists of two tasks. One is to design the classification scheme itself, and the other is to apply an existing scheme by allocating particular items to one or another of its categories. The actual work of most human classifiers is limited to the second task: they slot particular items in the categories of existing classificatory schemes. This is what the editors who classify judicial opinions according to the categories of the West key number system do, as well as the cataloguers who classify library materials in line with the Dewey Decimal or Library of Congress systems. The most prominent line of research and development of automated classification has been the attempt to design computer applications to do that too.

According to Koch, Day, et al. (1997:34), "the most important project in the area of automatic classification is OCLC's research project Scorpion." It adopts as its scheme the human-devised Dewey Decimal system and aims to classify Web sites and other electronic documents automatically according to its categories. It works by comparing "input documents" with "concept documents." Concept documents are electronic records containing words and phrases describing the subject for each category in the Dewey classification scheme. Input documents are Web sites or other electronic documents to be classified. Scorpion compares the words and phrases (weighted according to their richness of content, frequency, and position) in an input document with all concept documents and classifies it in the category or categories to which it bears a preset degree of similarity (Subramanian and Shafer 1997). Other experimental systems, such as KeyConcept, also work by comparing input and concept documents (Ravindran and Gauch 2004; Gauch, Chaffee, and Pretschner 2002).

At first glance this looks like a recapitulation of what human classifiers do when they compare the content of a particular document with the descriptions of categories in the classification scheme and place it in the category where it fits best. But actually it is a form of indexing, the difference being precisely the one that distinguishes classifying from indexing as they were defined at the start of this chapter. The human classifier assimilates the specific to the general by comparing the specifics of the document to be classified in question with the general categories of the scheme. This is the essence of classification. Programs such as Scorpion, on the other hand, compare one set of specific things (the contents of the input document) with other sets of specific things (the contents of the concept documents) and make their decisions on the basis of matches between particular terms. They remain entirely with the relations between particulars. This is the essence of indexing.

Scorpion's results have been good but not perfect, and human review is needed to weed out misclassifications (Hickey and Vizine-Goetz 1999). The reason, I believe, lies in the differences between programs such as Scorpion as elaborations of indexing rather than true mirrors of human classification procedures. Keith Shafer, designer of Scorpion, wrote: "While Scorpion cannot replace human cataloging, Scorpion can produce tools that help reduce the cost of traditional cataloging by automating subject assignment when items are available electronically. For instance, a list of potential subjects could be presented by Scorpion to a human cataloger who could then choose the most appropriate subject" (Shafer 1997).

Scorpion has remained an experimental project. Being unavailable to the public, one cannot evaluate how it works in practice. Northern Light (http://www.northernlight.com), however, seems to work on similar principles. This is a once-popular search engine that fell on hard times.[4] The following refers to Northern Light as it was in late 2002, when anyone could search it. As with other search engines, Northern Light retrieves documents on the basis of matches with the terms in users' queries, presented in order of relevance to the query. Northern Light's distinctive feature is that it then sorts the results into subject categories and presents them in "Custom Search Folders."

The folders represent a human-constructed classification scheme of over 200,000 categories derived from the Dewey Decimal system and the Library of Congress Subject Headings, with sixteen top-level subjects heading taxonomic hierarchies varying from depths of seven to nine levels (Notess 1998; Ward 1999). Northern Light automatically sorts the results of each search by comparing the words (weighted for importance in various ways) contained in each document returned by the search query with terms from controlled vocabularies established for each of the subject categories (Ward 1999; see also Notess 1998; http://www.northernlight.com/docs/search_help_folders.html, accessed March 20, 2002).[5] Although many of the technical details are proprietary and not publicly divulged, this seems to be the same as Scorpion's procedure of comparing input documents with concept documents.

Results of a search are returned in up to eighty folders. They bear the names of categories in the Northern Light classification scheme, and they are intended to enable searchers to identify by subject the located documents that are most likely to satisfy their needs. Clicking on a subject folder produces the search results classified under that subject, plus a new set of folders representing subtopics of that subject. For example, if the folder "psychology" is returned in a search, then clicking on it produces a screen with other folders, such as "social psychology" and other divisions of psychology. Opening one of them produces the search results classified under that subtopic, along with a new set of folders at the next lower level. One can continue that process until the hierarchical levels are exhausted.

Numerous trials that I ran showed that documents with high relevance ratings contained in the first folders presented tended to be quite germane to the query. However, major differences from how a human classifier would proceed become increasingly evident as one plunges deeper into the list of folders. For example, the twenty-first folder presented in a search for "social anthropology" on December 14, 2002, was "British pound." That folder contained fourteen items, most of which were reviews of anthropological books. They were classified in the folder "British pound" because those reviews all specified the cost of the books in pounds sterling. Clearly, Northern Light's automated classifier does not have the capacity to weed out similarities between documents that would be deemed irrelevant by a human classifier.

On the other hand, Northern Light often fails to classify items in categories that human classifiers would certainly select. A search for "lemurs" on December 11, 2002, produced 1,175 items. One of the folders generated by that search is "lemurs." This and other trials suggest that when a search query is identical to a category in the Northern Light classification scheme, one of the folders produced will be for that category. But the "lemurs" folder generated by the search query "lemurs" contained only nineteen items, under 2% of the total found in the search. Obviously the vast majority of items returned for the search query "lemurs" did not qualify for inclusion in the folder of the same name. Indeed, of the first twenty items listed most relevant to the search query, only three of them were found in the folder "lemurs" generated by that search. The omission of five others is understandable, because they concern the New York software company Lemur Networks, but the other twelve obviously pertain to the animal and would unquestionably be included in the category "lemurs" by a human classifier. These trials demonstrate that, in practice, Northern Light's automated classification function is severely limited when measured by human standards.

The reason, as with Scorpion, is that artificial intelligence is limited to the indexing procedures of specific matches and cannot recapitulate the judgments relating specifics to generalities that are the stuff of human classification. Northern Light inappropriately delivers "British pound" as a category of "social anthropology" because the terms that appear in a certain number of documents returned in a search for "social anthropology" match terms in the controlled vocabulary or concept document for "British pound" in Northern Light's classification scheme. It fails to include many documents appropriately found in a search for the keyword "lemurs" in the folder "lemurs" because the number or location of the terms in those documents does not sufficiently match the terms in the controlled vocabulary or concept document for "lemurs" in the classificatory scheme.

Another problem is that artificial intelligence has difficulty dealing with synonyms, homonyms, metaphors, and meanings carried more by context than by particular words. To computers, words such as "plant" and "tree" are simply strings of symbols, while to human beings they are meaningful signs. For humans, "plant" has several distinct meanings, one being "factory," another being a certain category of biological organisms, and a third being a verb meaning to place a seed in the ground (or, by metaphorical extension, an idea in someone's mind, etc.). "Tree" too has multiple meanings, one of them being a subcategory of "plant" in the second sense. Numerous techniques for sorting out such differences in automated contexts have been devised, such as examining other nearby words to determine the probability of which meaning of a homonym is intended. For instance, if "plant" occurs in close textual proximity to "industrial," then it is likely that it means "factory," while proximity to "tropical" indicates that its meaning as a biological organism is in play. This is not a sure bet, however, for some texts speak of the shrubs, trees, and other plants in industrial parks, while others discuss the special challenges of heating, ventilation, and air conditioning in (industrial) plants located in the tropics.

If, however, computers could be "taught" the meanings of words and phrases and ways to know when a term is used metaphorically or which homonym is intended, then they could manipulate them more effectively. Such is the intention of certain projects now in the research and development stage. The Cyc Project is engaged in building a knowledge base of millions of commonsense propositions, initially articulated by human analysts and then stored so as to be accessible by computers (Reed and Lenat 2002). Among those propositions are many dealing with the taxonomic relations among things, such as carrots and beans are kinds of vegetables, jellybeans are a kind of candy (and not a kind of vegetable), and so on.[6]

In a related area of development, the Semantic Web aims to enable computers to recognize differences between all kinds of things and concepts by labeling each with its unique "Uniform Resource Indicator" (URI). The familiar Uniform Resource Locators (URLs) for Web sites and e-mail addresses are kinds of URIs, so the URI for the University of Kansas could be www.ku.edu and the URI for the author of this book could be hanson@ku.edu. Everything else would have its own URI: one for "plant" in the sense of "factory," another for "plant" in the sense of a kind of biological organism, one for "tree" in the sense of a hierarchical, taxonomic structure, and so on. URIs also would be given to relationship terms such as "is larger than," "is a kind of," and "is married to." Then expressions called Resource Description Framework (RDF) "triples" could be devised to specify relationships among URIs, much as subjects and predicates do in ordinary sentences. When written in an appropriate machine-readable language such as XML (eXtensible Markup Language), expressions such as "The Middle Ages preceded the Scientific Revolution," "Russia is larger than Liechtenstein," or "A tree is a kind of plant" could be processed by and communicated between computers. It also would be possible for computers to conduct inferences based on such expressions. For example, from the propositions "An oak is a kind of tree" and "A tree is a kind of plant," the computer could automatically generate the further proposition "An oak is a kind of plant" (Berners-Lee, Hendler, and Lassila 2002, Schwartz 2002). If they can be perfected and brought into general use, developments such as the Cyc Project and the Semantic Web may eventually enable computers to recognize synonyms, homonyms, metaphors, and relationships between specific and general much as human beings do in ordinary discourse. This would represent a major step toward the capacity of artificial intelligence to simulate human classifying procedures. At the present time, however, these procedures are not in general use and thus have no discernable social consequences.

CAN ARTIFICIAL INTELLIGENCE CREATE CLASSIFICATORY SCHEMES?

Classification, as noted earlier, involves two distinct tasks. One is to design or devise classificatory schemes and the other is to allocate particular items to the categories of such schemes after they have been devised. In their efforts to mirror human intelligence, applications such as Scorpion and Northern Light attempt to automate the second task but not the first. Two other approaches initially seem to automate both tasks. What is especially interesting about them is that they do so while holding fast to the unique capabilities of artificial intelligence and make no attempt to emulate human intelligence.

HITS (Hyperlink-Induced Topic Search) operates specifically with Web sites. This ingenious technique was devised by Jon Kleinberg to avoid ambiguity in automatic Web searches. To explain how it works by example, a Web search for the keyword "jaguar" produces, among others, many sites about a brand of automobile, others about a kind of feline mammal, and still others about an Apple Mac operating system.[7] As with Google's technique for ranking the results of a Web search, HITS keys off of hyperlinks between sites. The reasoning behind HITS is that sites about the computer operating system are more likely to link to each other than they are to sites about the car or the cat. Automatically assessing all of the links among Web sites located with the search query "jaguar" reveals three groupings defined by frequency of reciprocal citations, corresponding to the three meanings of the term. The groupings or categories generated by analyzing hyperlinks can be sorted at several levels of similarity, thus distinguishing between sites dealing with entirely different topics, broadly similar topics, or closely related topics, such as pro-life and pro-choice persuasions in Web sites dealing with abortion (Hits and Misses 1998). Thus HITS seems capable of generating a hierarchical, taxonomic classification of Web sites returned by a search query, although I will argue in a moment that this is not exactly the case. The basic idea behind HITS is being developed and enhanced in the Clever Project (Chakrabarti et al. 1998).

Another procedure, called "clustering," also aims to identify more or less closely related groupings of documents. It achieves this by analyzing the contents of documents themselves rather than the hyperlinks between them. How clustering works becomes clear from a comparison with Scorpion. As discussed already, Scorpion compares the text of an "input document" with the texts of each of the "concept documents" that have been prepared in advance for every category in a classification system and classifies the input document in the category or categories to which it bears the greatest similarity. In clustering, no canonical concept documents are used to serve as standards for comparison. Instead, all of the documents in a set are compared for similarities to each other, two by two. This divides the set into clusters of similar documents (Subramanian and Shafer 1997).[8] Because the degree of similarity between document pairs is expressed quantitatively, one can identify a few broad clusters on the basis of general similarity or, within them, narrower clusters defined by higher degrees of similarity. One also can map the clusters, at any level of generality, according to their distance from each other. The result looks very much like a hierarchical, taxonomic classification of documents.

Clustering is in common use, being an important feature of the popular metasearch engines Vivisimo, Excite, Dogpile, MetaCrawler, and WebCrawler. These submit the user's keyword query to several search engines (such as Google, Lycos, Looksmart, AltaVista) and present the top results from each. Using the "preferences" function, the user can set Vivisimo to return a total of about 100, 200, or 500 results, the default setting being about 200. As of August 2005, searches on the other metasearch engines usually returned less than 100 results. In addition to being presented in the standard search engine format as a relevance-weighted list, the findings are automatically grouped into categories on the basis of the clustering technology just described. Vivisimo, the only one to describe its procedure, generates its clusters using the two-to-three-line summaries of each site provided by the several search engines it consults to locate them.[9] There is some hierarchy, but not particularly deep. In most cases the clusters contain Web sites with no subcategories. Some clusters are further divided at one level, a few at two, and I found one at three levels in a Vivisimo search for "psychology" on February 24, 2004.

Unlike HITS, which relies on hyperlinks and is therefore limited largely to Web sites, clustering can be used to sort digitalized documents of any sort. Anyone can use Vivisimo's advance search function, for example, to get clustered search results of the PubMed database of medical literature, the *New York Times*, eBay, and several other databases. It also markets its clustering engine as a way to help organizations bring order to their large volumes of poorly organized memos, files, and reports.

As techniques to sort documents at several hierarchical levels of similarity, clustering and HITS seem to bear all of the markings of taxonomic classification. However, a crucial difference divides them from human-generated, textual mode taxonomic schemes. And it is precisely that: the latter are *schemes*. That is, they are structured categories that have been laid down in advance and into which documents, Web sites, and things of any description are classified. Clustering and HITS do not use predefined categories. They begin with a concrete array of documents and sort them into ad hoc categories according to their degrees of similarity to each other.[10]

This may not seem fundamentally different from human classification. After all, oral and textual mode taxonomic schemes have to begin *somewhere*, and their beginnings are not unlike clustering. One or more human beings observe an array of objects, perceive degrees of similarity among them, and sort them into categories accordingly. But the difference is this: the human scheme becomes a classificatory framework into which new items are subsequently slotted, and if its categories seem to make good sense and it can successfully accommodate quite a lot of new items, then it becomes institutionalized and considerable pressure is exerted to fit more and more items into it. It becomes, in a word, a part of culture. It gets incorporated into the preestablished framework that culture establishes for the ordering and understanding of things and experiences.

HITS and clustering differ drastically from this, because they never form lasting schemes. Their categories are created afresh with each inspection of an array, and they do not survive that inspection. Hence, they remain entirely ad hoc, never forming lasting categories into which future items may be classified. One can observe this firsthand by watching the metasearch engines listed earlier at work. On February 24, 2004, I ran two searches for "American civil war generals" on Dogpile, within minutes of each other. Although the queries were identical, the first search returned fifty-five Web sites and the second sixty-four. The explanation is that different numbers of findings were reported from some of the search engines consulted, because the allotted time ran out or for some other reason. Most interesting, not only do the numbers of results change, but so do the categories into which they are clustered. Both of the searches returned clusters titled "Soldiers," "Pictures," and several others. But "Confederate," which with seven sites was the largest cluster to emerge from the first trial, did not appear at all in the second trial. Nor did "Reenactment, Gettysburg," a cluster with three sites in the first trial. In revenge, the three-site cluster "Army, Major" appeared in the second trial but not the first. The same sort of thing happened when I performed the identical search with Vivisimo.

The reason for variations such as this is that clustering and HITS do not attempt to mimic the kind of classification born of human intelligence that subsumes specifics under generalities. Instead, they utilize artificial intelligence's strong point, most obvious in keyword searching, of matching specifics. In HITS, the specifics are hyperlinks to and from Web sites; in clustering, they are the contents of documents. The same principles operate in both, but it will be simpler to confine this brief analysis of how they work to clustering. Keyword searching is a kind of indexing. Its aim is to locate items in a database that match the terms of a search query. The query may be as short as a single number or word, it may be a set of terms conditioned by Boolean operators and proximity controls, or it may be indefinitely long: a sentence, an entire page of text, or whatever. Clustering, we have seen, works by comparing all documents in a data set, two by two. This too is a form of matching, or indexing. It is as if each document in the data set was considered a keyword query used to search all of the others. But the critical difference is that in an ordinary keyword search, only documents having exact matches with the query will be returned. With clustering, because an entire document is used as a search query, no other document in the data set will be an exact match for it. But some documents will be closer to it than others, as determined by the familiar ranking criteria such as the number of shared words and the importance and location of those words. Thus in clustering, the search is for approximate rather than exact matches between whole documents. Clustering uses the degrees of similarity among documents in the set to group them into categories, often with hierarchical levels. And yet, because there are no predetermined categories, it is not really classifying. At bottom, both keyword searching and clustering depend on weighted matching, and therefore they should be understood as variations on the single technique of indexing.

In the automated mode of information management, artificial intelligence processes information stored in artificial memory. What I wish to stress about clustering is that, unlike the other applications we have examined, its use of artificial intelligence does not attempt to mimic human intelligence. Scorpion and Northern Light do try to recapitulate the human way of classifying by subsuming particulars into preestablished general categories represented by their control documents or controlled vocabularies. But, as I have argued already, that objective is doomed to failure in principle, because the control documents are not really general but just other particulars. Thus they compare particulars to each other, which is indexing and not human-style classifying. For its part, clustering also utilizes the unique indexing capacity of artificial intelligence to match particulars. But, because it does not take any documents to be definitive of preestablished categories, the groupings it generates—and the relations among those groupings—are freshly created for each search. This is a distinctly new way of organizing information, unfettered by the categories of culture and fundamentally different from human techniques. Indeed, it would be nearly as difficult for human intelligence to organize information by clustering as it is for artificial intelligence to mimic the human way of classifying.

The most important point for our purposes is that creative techniques such as HITS and clustering, which develop automation's unique capacity to index instead of trying to ape human classifying powers, encourage a transition from a closed to an open culture. Indexing eschews those preconceived categories indigenous to classifying which, when they become dogmatic, are at the heart of the problem with culture. The next task is to explore in more detail how indexing, with its ad hoc, just-in-time method of organizing information, encourages creativity and an open frame of mind.

Chapter 7

The Automated Mode in Principle

In 1950, Alan Turing, a seminal figure in the field of artificial intelligence, devised a simple experiment to determine whether computers could think. Place a computer behind a screen or in a separate room and have it answer questions posed by a person. If the questioner cannot decide whether the answers are coming from a human being or a machine, then the computer can think. The Turing test is vividly representative of the early goal to make artificial intelligence simulate human intelligence to the greatest degree possible. A daunting goal, because the workings of human intelligence itself are poorly understood. Therefore, all that could be done was to try to design machines that, as in Turing's thought experiment, would generate outcomes indistinguishable from what human beings would produce for the same task or problem. But fundamental differences between the two raise serious questions as to whether, even in principle, artificial intelligence could ever simulate human intelligence (Dreyfus 1992). These differences convince Donald Norman that the goal of simulating human intelligence was a bad idea in the first place. "In general, humans can be characterized as pattern-recognizing, meaning-finding systems, excellent at interpreting information, finding meaning and explaining phenomena rapidly and efficiently," he wrote, while computers excel at the very different tasks of "numerical computation and anything that requires precision and repeatability" (Norman 1997).

Someone who imagines that artificial intelligence can eventually simulate human intelligence must assume that computers operate, or can be made to operate, in the same way as human thinking. It follows from this assumption that, given its speed and accuracy, artificial intelligence will eventually do what human intelligence does now, only better, and therefore may some day replace human intelligence. This is the stuff that anxiety or excitement about the prospect of computers taking over the world is made of. But those who agree with Norman and Dreyfus, that human and artificial intelligence are fundamentally different, are also likely to agree with Norman (1997), that "it should be possible to develop a symbiotic, complementary strategy for cooperative interaction" between the two forms of intelligence (see also Bolter 1984:234, 238). To my mind, this is the truly exciting (and not at all worrisome) prospect, for it anticipates that the power of information management can be significantly enhanced when the automated mode joins forces with the oral and textual modes.

If we consider information management a kind of thinking, then this view accepts the proposition that computers can think, but it does not follow that therefore artificial intelligence simulates human intelligence. Information management, as we have seen, requires both memory for storing information and intelligence for processing it in various ways. Humans are equipped with both memory and intelligence, and so they are indeed a kind of being that can think all by itself. That is precisely what happens in the oral mode of information management. Computers also have memory and intelligence (the artificial kind in both cases), so they too can think all by themselves. That is what happens in the automated mode of information management. But this does not mean that computers and humans think in the same way. The human mind is no more a kind of computer than computers are simulations of the human mind. But they do complement each other. As we shall see in chapter 9, a great deal of activity today, including thinking, is done by agencies incorporating various combinations of the automated, oral, and textual modes, each making its distinctive contribution to the overall process.

Framing the issue this way, the salient question becomes not so much whether computers can think as how they *participate in* thinking. This is a critical issue, for the most important development in information management in the last half century was the increasing role that the automated mode came to play in it. Artificial intelligence and human intelligence coordinate in a powerful, new kind of thinking that has transformed how information is organized and understood. And that, I maintain, has an impact on the evolution and fate of culture.

Computers have become central to thinking in two senses of that term. For one, they are central in importance. They have taken over many tasks that were performed, more slowly and laboriously, by human intelligence. This makes for greater economy of information management. It is analogous to what Gregory Bateson said about out how, in purely human thinking, certain routine functions get "sunk" in primary process (the unconscious), allowing secondary process (consciousness) to attend more efficiently to more complex tasks with contingent outcomes (Bateson 1972b:141–42). Thus learning to tie one's shoes or maintain balance on a bicycle takes all of one's concentration at first, but after these activities have been mastered, primary process takes them over. For this reason, it is possible to think about other things (what to have for breakfast, what to do first upon arriving at work or school) while tying one's shoes or riding a bicycle, but not while making decisions such as which shirt to wear. With automation, the same sort of thing happens. Certain tasks are sunk in (taken over by) artificial intelligence—performing mathematical calculations, scrutinizing large bodies of information for desired items, alphabetizing lists, and many others—freeing human intelligence to focus on other things. Years ago, for example, I had memorized about twenty telephone numbers of family members, friends, and organizations that I called frequently. Now I have sunk them in the automatic dial feature of my telephones and have only two or three of them memorized . . . mainly my own home and office numbers.

But more instructively, computers are central in the sense of being in the middle of a composite process that both begins and ends with human intelligence. The process of acquiring information begins with the formulation of the problem or query, which is fed to the computer for processing, and it ends with evaluation of the computer's results. The bookend tasks are both the province of human intelligence. It does not follow, however, that artificial intelligence just helps human beings do what they otherwise might have done, albeit more slowly and laboriously, by themselves. Instead, it is another example of Marshall McLuhan's notion that the medium is the message: from its central position, artificial intelligence changes everything. Most importantly, it creates an environment where people are stimulated to think "outside the box" instead of passively accepting received wisdom.

This is a function of the decline of classification and the ascent of indexing as the automated mode plays an increasingly prominent role in information management. The difference this makes is captured by Gilles

Deleuze's and Félix Guattari's distinction between arborescent (tree-like) and rhizomatic structures. "Unlike trees or their roots, the rhizome connects any point to any other point, and its traits are not necessarily linked to traits of the same nature. . . . In contrast to centered (even polycentric) systems with hierarchical modes of communication and preestablished paths, the rhizome is an acentered, nonhierarchical, nonsignifying system without a General and without an organizing memory or central automaton, defined solely by a circulation of states" (Deleuze and Guattari 1987:21). Classification is arborescent; we have already noted that the standard form of a taxonomy is an inverted tree.[1] Indexing (especially automated searching) is rhizomatic; it is noncentered and nonhierarchical. Indexing liberates thought and opens culture, because it is less bound by established categories and guidelines. Therefore, far from restricting the role of human intelligence, the participation of artificial intelligence actually challenges it to more creative activity.[2] This chapter and the next aim to unpack what it is about automation that fosters this greater open-mindedness. It comes down largely to three elements of automated information technology in widespread use: Internet communication, surfing the Web with hypertext, and automated searching.

INTERNET COMMUNICATION, HYPERTEXT, AND AUTOMATED SEARCHING

Internet Communication

Gary Shank and Donald Cunningham (1996) point out that list-servs, chat, and other forms of Internet communication foster a particularly creative form of thinking. The openness of these discussion forums invites participants from a variety of backgrounds. This produces diverse contributions which, taken together, transcend standard classificatory categories and traditional disciplinary boundaries. Discussion participants who would make sense of such unruly collections of ideas engage in "abductive" thinking, "whereby we, when confronted with some experience not accounted for by our existing beliefs, invent a new set of beliefs or revise an existing one" (p. 36). Shank (1993) characterizes such opportunistic foraging for meaning as follows: "The abductive researcher is less like an experimenter and . . . more of a hunter-gatherer. He/she learns to gather information and combine that information in bricolage fashion. These unique and interdisciplinary craftings of ideas and facts allow the researcher to work outside of strict theoretical boundaries, and to turn to the world of experience directly for guidance. Given the wealth of information available to the hunter-gatherer on the Net (3,000-plus lists on Bitnet alone), it should be no surprise that the virtual scholarly community will evolve individuals who will thrive on being able to juxtapose and combine seemingly disparate threads of information in order to yield new and exciting venues of insights."

These characteristics make Internet communication extraordinarily fertile field for the production of creative thought. "All one has to do is to toss out a new insight, and more than likely a new thread will develop" (Shank 1993). Sometimes this even occurs by accident. Shank and Cunningham (1996:38) give the example of a member of an educational research list who inadvertently sent a private message about the need to keep a refrigerator door shut to the entire list. Although the sender immediately noticed the error and sent a message of apology to the list, other members took it as a metaphor for the current state of educational research, and a thread began with postings regarding the contents of the educational refrigerator, how much energy is required to keep them cold, the inefficient seal on the refrigerator door, and so on.

Hypertext

Surfing the Web by hypertext often generates similarly unanticipated juxtapositions of information. The standard definition of hypertext is "any text that contains 'links' to other documents—words or phrases in the document that can be chosen by a reader and which cause another document to be retrieved and displayed."[3] The links are similar to footnotes and citations in print documents, but hypertext technology creates a massive difference in the way they can be used. Actually tracking down print citations is a laborious and time-consuming task requiring trips to the library to pull books and journals off the shelves. This cannot possibly duplicate the trains of thinking along webs of connections that automation makes possible through the capacity to open hyperlinked sites and documents with the click of a mouse. The medium is the message. Artificial intelligence and human intelligence symbiotically reinforce each other as they work in parallel fashion to jump by association from one site or one idea to another.

Charles Ess likens this effect to travel. Like the traveler who visits other countries, the Internet surfer encounters, in greatly accelerated fashion, a wide variety of new and different ways of thinking and doing things. This exposure broadens one's understanding of cultural differences, some of which one may adopt as preferable to one's own ways (Ess 2001:24). He perceives in the growth of computer-mediated communication "a hopeful model for the future of a global Internet, one which cuts between the usual dichotomies between utopia and dystopia and between global (and potentially imperialistic) and local (and potentially isolated) cultures. In this middle ground may emerge a pluralistic humanity—dual citizens and polybrids at home in both distinctive . . . local cultures and a global . . . online culture" (p. 28).

Hypertext transforms the way people acquire and use information. I interviewed several college-level English composition teachers about the ways in which students today go about conducting research and writing the results. All of them stated that research in automated sources, with its ease of following hyperlinks to jump between sites or from page to another within sites, fosters associative rather than linear thinking. One teacher said that "hierarchy is gone," because the "rhizomatic" character of automated research is to follow lateral networks of connections in any number of directions. This bursts the bonds of classificatory categories and exposes students to a greater diversity of information than is found in traditional, textual mode sources such as encyclopedias or textbooks. That can be confusing, and the papers students produce may be disjointed, but another teacher said it also "could be freeing for a lot of students . . . and wonderfully creative." Surfing along hyperlinks juxtaposes concepts and ideas in novel ways, suggesting new kinds of relations among the sites and stimulating searchers to develop new insights and understandings (Burbules and Callister 2000:44, 48).

Automated Searching

Keyword searching contains the same potential for creative thinking as Internet communication and hyperlink surfing, but it realizes it in quite different and even more powerful ways. Following hyperlinks or list-serv threads is a matter of going single file from one site or document or posting to another. Automated searching, in contrast, presents the user with a simultaneous array of multiple results, any one of which might be chosen.

Furthermore, automation plays a narrower role in Web surfing and Internet communication than in keyword searching. In all three cases, what artificial intelligence does is sandwiched between activities of human intelligence. With surfing in hypertext, the only step that is automated is the shift from one document or site to another when a hyperlink is clicked. The decision as to what words to hyperlink is made by the human Web designer, and the decision whether or not to follow any hyperlink is made by the human user. After artificial intelligence takes one to the hyperlinked document or site, the human intelligence of the searcher takes over again to decide if the new site contains anything of interest, to go back if it does not or, if it does, to ponder it and to consider following any of its hyperlinks to still other sites. An analogous situation obtains when following threads on list-servs, where mouse clicks take one to those postings that one wishes to read. With keyword searching, on the other hand, the searcher's human intelligence frames the query. Then artificial intelligence undertakes an operation of indexing that is much more complex than the simple opening of a hyperlinked site or a posting. It compares the query to documents in its database, selects those that match it, ranks them as more or less relevant to the query, and, if it organizes Web sites by HITS or includes a clustering engine such as Vivisimo, it groups the results in subject categories. At that point, human intelligence steps in again to evaluate the findings, consult some of them, redefine the search query, or whatever seems appropriate.

When compared to the classifications and print indexes indigenous to the textual mode, the automated searching process empowers information searchers in several ways. Most obvious is its speed, which makes it possible to consult hundreds or thousands of documents in seconds. Second is its scope. Many printed documents such as newspaper stories and works of fiction have not been indexed in any detailed way, and therefore are not subject to search. In contrast, any document or database in digitalized form can be electronically searched by keyword. And finally, in the textual mode, the process of information seeking is constrained from the outset by the categories of the classification scheme or the topics that constitute the index. Everyone has had the frustrating experience of finding such indexes too general or being unable to divine what terms the indexer selected for the topic of one's interest. Yet unless one is prepared to scan every page of every work, there is no choice but to follow the avenues of access to information that authors, catalogers, and indexers have laid down.

Keyword searching is not so constrained (Harrington 1984–1985: 546; Bowker and Star 1999:292; Bolter 1991:22; Richmond 1965:5). Automation enables users to design their own queries and research strategies. In effect, every keyword search creates a new index, tailored to its particular query, of the text, catalog, Internet, or other database being searched. The search may be novel and unprecedented, conducted according to queries that have never been framed before. Which sites, cases, books, or articles emerge will depend entirely on the topic as stipulated in the query. It is not even sensible to speak of a "topic" as having any enduring presence, because what passes as such, when specified electronically, expands, contracts, and is reconfigured according to any number of diverse criteria used to design the specific search query. In 1984, David Bolter imagined what might result if the contents of books were made available in electronic form . . . something that is in fact occurring today. "The electronic medium would open up new ways to look, suggest new questions, and make at least some new answers possible. . . . It would allow the reader to treat written knowledge as a vast workspace in which to build his own interpretive structures" (Bolter 1984:230).

One of the first applications that made these capabilities available to a large population of users was the computerized legal research service LEXIS, which has been on the market since 1973. It will be described in detail in the next chapter. For now, I want to unpack how the automated indexing procedures at the heart of LEXIS and, today, many other systems in general use, affect the research process, and why. John Henry Merryman grasped the crucial point as early as 1977 when he wrote: "One of the most attractive features of the LEXIS system . . . is that it liberates the researcher from [preestablished] indexes and opens up an enormous range of possible avenues of access to the literature" (1977:426). Tim Berners-Lee extended the same point to the World Wide Web when he wrote: "The vision I have for the web is about anything being potentially connected with anything. It is a vision that provides us with new freedom, and allows us to grow faster than we ever could when we were fettered by the hierarchical classification systems into which we bound ourselves" (Berners-Lee 1999:1–2).

Actually, automated searching liberates research in two quite different ways. They both represent advantages over the preestablished categories of classifications and indexes in the textual mode, but they work in opposite directions. One of them, focused searching, tightens automated indexing for greater precision; the other, open-ended searching, loosens it for more flexibility and imaginative interpretation.

FOCUSED SEARCHING

Focused searching pertains to the capacity to frame index terms in ways that pinpoint particular issues and questions with great specificity. This is especially useful to searchers who already know precisely the kind of information they want. For example, as I was writing an earlier chapter of this book, I thought it would be useful to include the given name of the Dalgarno in whose philosophical language garlic and onions are named nebghnagbana and nebghnagmuba. I "Googled" the name Dalgarno (Google has become so popular that a new verb has been coined for searching with it), and in a minute or two I found that the name I was seeking was George. A trip to the library to consult textual mode sources would have taken much longer, and I might well have decided that knowing this information was not worth the effort to get it.

Focused searchers can design highly specific queries, using Boolean operators AND and NOT and other restricting devices to limit results to those that satisfy a narrow set of criteria. This enables them to sort rapidly through databases of any size to locate items directly on point. People often search in this way to locate specific passages, at least part of which they already know verbatim. As a brief trial, consider how focused searching might be used for a research interest of mine in a very narrow topic: the cultural significance of symmetry in New Zealand Maori rafter patterns (see e.g., Hanson 1983). On March 8, 2004, I entered the query "culture AND maori AND rafter AND symmetry" on several search engines and databases to find any material specifically on the topic. Google displayed sixteen results, and Vivisimo returned forty-six findings in one trial and thirty-nine in another.[4] Many of the results were irrelevant, because the search terms appeared in them in unrelated ways. Most of the others had to do with the mathematics of symmetry as manifested in Maori rafter patterns; there was very little on their connection with the larger Maori culture. Turning to the more academic databases Expanded Academic Index, ArticleFirst, and WorldCat, none of them returned any findings at all for the full query. ArticleFirst did not give results even when I expanded my queries as far as "maori AND symmetry" or "maori AND rafter." WorldCat was almost as disappointing, with no results for "maori AND symmetry" and two for "maori AND rafter." Expanded Academic Index found six articles for "maori AND rafter" and one very useful article for "maori AND symmetry AND rafter*."[5] Despite numerous irrelevancies and redundancies and the paucity of results, the searches did turn up a few important documents that I definitely would need to consult were I doing active research on the subject.

Focused automated searching actually is a variation on textual mode research via classification, for to say that focused searchers know exactly what information they want is to say that they are already quite sure how that information fits in what they are doing. That is, as with research in the textual mode, the contexts or categories are set in advance. Automated searching liberates the searcher in this situation in the sense that it is much faster, as in my search for George Dalgarno. It also makes it possible to define the search more precisely than can be done with textual mode resources, for print classifications and indexes do not organize information with a sufficient degree of specificity to handle questions as narrow as the one about the cultural associations of symmetry in Maori rafter patterns. Finally, automation allows researchers to design their own focused search queries rather than having to rely on the preset categories in print classifications and indexes. In sum, focused automated procedures enable researchers with very specific questions to use customized queries to seek information directly relevant to their purposes more specifically, extensively, and rapidly than is possible with the prefabricated classifications and indexes of the textual mode.

OPEN-ENDED SEARCHING

The liberation stemming from automated open-ended searching is entirely different, and more pertinent to our general argument. It is in play when researchers are in the process of learning about something but have not yet finalized their interpretation of it. In these circumstances, they may frame quite general queries, including using the Boolean operator OR, to achieve a broad range of results. This is likely to turn up a great deal of irrelevant material, but among the findings there also may be nuggets that prove pertinent in unforeseen ways. Pondering them may generate new insights and stimulate the searcher to form creative new interpretations. To explain how this works requires a brief excursion into information theory.

In this context, the term *information* will be used in a more technical sense than heretofore. Thus far I have used it in its colloquial sense, essentially meaning "data," and often serving as a synonym for knowledge. In information theory, the term has a very different meaning. "Information" is the degree of unpredictablility in a message. This is one of three components of any message, the other two being redundancy (its degree of predictability) and noise (unintended signals that creep into the message, such as static on the radio or stuttering in speech). We will not consider noise further, but it is important to recognize that information and redundancy vary inversely. The response "fine" to the question "How are you?" is highly predictable. Therefore, that message is saturated with redundancy and carries virtually no information. On the other hand, the response "walnut" to the same question is much less predictable, and thus it is high in information and low in redundancy.

The intelligibility of messages is a function of their redundancy. The more redundancy, the greater the intelligibility. When people say "fine" upon being asked how they are, it is easy to understand what is meant. It is not, as a matter of fact, necessarily a true description of the person's condition, but everyone understands it as the stock answer to the question, which conveys politeness and the willingness to continue the conversation while not inviting further inquiries into one's precise state of health or well-being. A message high in information, on the other hand, is considerably less intelligible. If the question "How are you?" elicits the response "walnut," then we are at a loss as to what is meant and uncertain about how to proceed, if at all, with the conversation.

Messages extremely high in redundancy are so predictable that we learn nothing new from them. Those extremely high in information are so unpredictable that we can make nothing of them and, therefore, we learn nothing from them either. The most interesting messages lie in between: those with enough redundancy to be intelligible and enough information that we can learn something new from them. If, for example, someone responds to "How are you?" with "The heart is a lonely hunter," then the meaning is not immediately apparent, but it is interesting enough to invite us to think further about it, and it is not difficult to come up with a few possibilities that tell us something about the person's condition that we had not known before.

These considerations from information theory are relevant to the argument of this book in at least two ways. For one, people often seek the familiar because messages high in redundancy are comfortable, while those high in information can be disconcerting or threatening. Messages so high in information as to be entirely unintelligible are mildly annoying, because we can make no sense of them, but typically we dismiss them quickly and move on. More threatening are messages with sufficient redundancy to be intelligible, but with enough information that understanding them demands the extra effort of thinking in unfamiliar channels. Threatening because, at the very least, they require overcoming the inertia of established ideas. At most, they challenge established ideas and propose a more or less radical change in worldview. An example is how familiar propositions, or messages, about God or the church sometimes take on a radically new meaning. In some cases this generates considerable turmoil as they come to the painful conclusion that they can no longer abide by the dogmas with which they grew up. In others, it is the transforming experience of acquiring new religious belief and fervor. The extent of that change is graphically captured by the notion of being "born again."

Information and redundancy are relative terms. Because we start from different places, what is redundant to you may be information to me. Redundancy to born-again Christians or inveterate gardeners is information to atheists or machinists, and vice versa. This is actually another way of articulating what I have called the trouble with culture. The concepts and customs of one's own culture have high redundancy, while those from other cultures are more or less high in information. Most people, most of the time are uncomfortable with very much information in the ideas they entertain, because, as I have said, new and different ways of thinking and behaving require effort to understand and may be threatening. People tend to become defensive, and even hostile, when confronted with ideas and messages high enough in information to challenge their standard ones. This is the stuff of intolerance and culture wars. As we have seen in chapter 2, the automation of information makes it easy to immerse oneself in narrowcasted television channels, Web sites, and discussion groups that reinforce what is familiar (highly redundant) and to reject or ignore anything else. This is most likely to occur among people who select their sources of conversation, news, and other information more to fit comfortably with what they already think than to alert them to unfamiliar ideas and procedures from which they might learn something new.

But the other point of relevance of information theory to our exploration of automation cuts in the opposite direction. People who want to expand their knowledge, whether for professional purposes or out of plain curiosity, value automation for its capacity to uncover ideas that are relatively high in information. Taking such ideas seriously and making the necessary effort to understand them often results in new insights and problem solutions. This open-minded attitude is conducive to tolerance. Used in this way, as it often is, automation serves to lessen the trouble with culture and calm the culture wars.

We can develop this point via the distinctions that we have drawn between textual mode searching, focused automated searching, and open-ended automated searching. New insights and innovative ideas stem from messages located at the high information end of the intelligible range. Such ideas are more likely to be born of open-ended automated searching than from either research in the textual mode or focused automated searching. Sources for textual mode research, organized as they are in terms of preestablished categories and well-trodden paths of thinking that human catalogers and classifiers are mandated to follow, tend to yield results quite high in redundancy. Those who are beginning to learn a subject are fed standardized material, and even advanced researchers circle largely within a predefined field of knowledge, adding small parts to it but rarely reconceptualizing it in original ways.

Redundancy also is key to automated searching, but in a more mechanical way. Automated searches seek matches with the query, and two things that match, being identical, are perfectly redundant. When a research query is formulated in a narrowly focused way, as in the earlier example of symmetry in Maori rafter patterns, relatively few documents contain matches with the query, and the probability is great that those documents will be highly redundant both with each other and with the research interest that prompted the query in the first place. That, of course, serves the purposes of focused searching, that is, to confirm something that one is already quite sure of, to fill small gaps, or to find new contributions to a familiar body of knowledge.

Open-ended automated searching also operates by means of matches with the query, and in that sense it too involves redundancy. However, search queries that are framed as general topics, or that encompass more than one topic by using the Boolean operator OR, will turn up a plethora of findings that will differ more from each other and diverge more widely from the predefined research interest that prompted the query than the results of a focused search. A number of those findings will be high in information. Indeed, the information level of some of them may be so high as to render their connection to the research interest unintelligible. They are dismissed as "garbage." But certain other results have sufficient redundancy to signal a glimmering of intelligibility: they seem to fit the query somehow, although just how is not immediately apparent. This stimulates the researcher to try to imagine what the connection might be, and that can lead to innovative ideas. In this way, open-ended automated searching liberates human intelligence by stimulating it to use its interpretive powers to the fullest extent.

To test these propositions, I undertook trial searches with general queries on a few topics that I already knew enough about to be able to distinguish between findings that were directly relevant (high redundancy), entirely irrelevant (extremely high information), and possibly relevant, but in ways not immediately apparent (somewhat high information). My hypothesis was that the findings that were somewhat high in information would be most likely to stimulate new ways of thinking about the topic described by the query. In contrast to my narrowly focused query about Maori rafter patterns, I made these open-ended so as to turn up findings that would cover a wide range between high redundancy and high information. The queries I selected were "Tuamotu OR Tuamotuan" (an archipelago of atolls east of Tahiti), "Clifford Geertz" (a well-known contemporary anthropologist), and "cultural relativism" (an anthropological and philosophical position discussed in chapter 3).

First I ran the trials using the search engine Google. The results were massive: nearly 34,000 for Clifford Geertz, 55,000 for "Tuamotu OR Tuamotuan," and 107,000 for cultural relativism. These were weighted for relevance, but because I was interested in finding sites high in information (technical sense) that might stimulate new insights, I reviewed sites with low as well as high rankings. Their sheer number made it impractical to look at each one, so I glanced quickly at one page of ten, jumped ahead about 100 sites, scanned that page, jumped ahead another 100, and so on. This exercise caused me to lose some confidence in Google's ranking function, for many of the sites buried 500 or more deep in the results for "cultural relativism" seemed no less pertinent to the topic than those at the head of the list.[6] I also wondered what the point is of announcing that tens or hundreds of thousands of sites are located for various searches, because the maximum that I could get Google to display for each of the three searches was 1,000. (Similarly, a search for "Tuamotu

OR Tuamotuan" on Altavista located about 17,500 sites, but, like Google, it ceased displaying them after 1,000.) I left the Google trials with the sense that a search engine of that sort is especially valuable for focused automated searching: locating items in extremely large databases that precisely match specific queries. It is less useful for the more general queries associated with the open-ended searching, because sifting through more than the first twenty or so of the overwhelming flood of results soon becomes tedious. Thus it is easy to miss items high in information (technical sense) buried more deeply in the findings that may stimulate the searcher to think about the topic in new ways.

I ran another set of trials on the meta-search engine Vivisimo. This gave many fewer results—for example, 142 for "cultural relativism" as opposed to the 107,000 for that query on Google. Despite the much smaller numbers, in actual practice, Vivisimo's clustering feature enables one to review more sites than one would normally visit in a Google search. Looking at the thirty clustering headings in the results for "cultural relativism" gives one a preliminary sense of the aspects of the topic treated by most of the 142 sites returned by the search.[7] One can then go quickly to those sites that seem relevant or interesting. It is rare, on the other hand, to consult anywhere near 100 sites in a search with Google or some other nonclustering engine, regardless of the total number of sites it finds.

In some cases the machine-generated clusters make little sense in human terms. The 142 findings returned for the query "cultural relativism" that I ran on Vivisimo on February 29, 2004, included, for example, a cluster of four called "remote name" and another cluster of two labeled "next message." Both of these clusters consisted of messages about cultural relativism posted to online discussion groups. In the heading of each of the messages in the first group was a line labeled "remote name" followed by a long number. The heading of each message in the second group contained a line reading "next message," followed by a hyperlinked author name and message subject. Those cluster titles—"remote name" and "next message"—had nothing to do with the content of the messages about cultural relativism. I wondered, indeed, why there was not another cluster called "previous message," because a line with that title also appeared in the heading of both messages in the "next message" cluster.

Usually, however, the clusters do identify content. Most of the time these are what one would expect, or, in more technical terms, high in redundancy. In response to the query about cultural relativism, for example, these included predictable clusters labeled "ethics," "ethnocentrism," idea," and "tolerance, moral." But sometimes the clusters are unexpected enough (high enough in information) to arouse curiosity. Thus the small cluster titled "Pitcairn Island" that appeared in my search for "Tuamotu OR Tuamotuan" interested me, because Pitcairn Island is not part of the Tuamotu archipelago. Opening the sites in that cluster, I was intrigued to learn of a legal case that has been going on since 1999, in which thirteen men (out of a total population of forty-seven) have been charged with sexual abuse and assault. Wondering how a society with a population of under fifty could persist (especially with virtually all of its adult males under indictment), and whether it was time for another anthropological study to be conducted there, I followed some of the hyperlinks to view photographs of the island and its people and to learn a bit more about life there.

After a half hour or so of informative browsing, I decided I had better get on with my main task, and I left Pitcairn Island to conduct another Vivisimo search for Clifford Geertz. Among its 130 or so findings was a five-site cluster "ethnocentrism." Most of the sites in it pertained to an article by Keith Windschuttle titled "The Ethnocentrism of Clifford Geertz," published in *The New Criterion* in October 2002. Intrigued, because I had never thought of Geertz as a particularly ethnocentric fellow, I read the article on one of the sites that had its full text. It included a discussion of Geertz's reaction to comments made by Claude Lévi-Strauss regarding the tendency of different cultural strains within diverse, contemporary societies to distinguish themselves and claim superiority over the others. This struck me as fitting very well with my own argument in this book regarding the divisive workings of culture in contemporary society, and I incorporated it in my discussion (it appears at the start of chapter 2).

Finishing the article, I once again chastised myself for straying from my main task and focused my thoughts back to how using a tool such as Vivisimo affected the research process. Then, with a start, I realized that what I had been thinking of as diversions turned out to be exactly the effect I was interested in exploring. I had encountered items that were unpredictable, high in information: "Why Pitcairn? It's not in the Tuamo-tus." "Geertz ethnocentric? I don't think so." Not so unpredictable, however, as to be unintelligible: Pitcairn is located not far from the Tuamotus; Geertz is associated with ethnocentrism, although more by way of criti-cizing it than representing it. When curiosity provoked me to look further,

I learned some new and interesting things (about the charges against Pitcairn Island men), and I found something relevant to me (Lévi-Strauss on cultural diversity) in a way entirely different from the original purpose of the search. Although I make no claim that these qualify as outbursts of creativity, they are made of the same stuff: thoughts stimulated by the encounter with unanticipated material relatively high in information.

Of the trials I attempted, Vivisimo proved more productive than Google of automation's capacity to provoke new thinking in open-ended searches. Google's presentation of results in a simple if interminable list does not draw attention to anything particular about them other than an assessment of their relevance to the search query as reflected by their position in the list. The clustering feature of a metasearch engine such as Vivisimo, on the other hand, adds something new. It works as if the search query had been refined with another term connected by the Boolean operator AND. Thus the cluster on Pitcairn Island in my Tuamotu search is rather like making the query "Tuamotu AND Pitcairn," and the ethnocentrism cluster in the other search is as if the search query had been "Clifford Geertz AND ethnocentrism."[8] But because the cluster names are generated automatically, they may signal aspects of the search results that users would not have thought of themselves. This does not happen often, because most of the clusters are so predictable (high in redundancy) that they do not attract any particular attention, while others are so high in information as to be unintelligible and therefore useless (as with "remote name" and "next message" in one of my Vivisimo searches). But a few are both unanticipated and interesting enough to invite the human analyst to reflect on them. This encourages thinking "outside the box" about the topic, and that is what leads to new insights into it. Vivisimo itself makes this point in promoting its clustering engine as a means of organizing the archive of documents produced by businesses or other organizations: "The value lies in navigating and grasping the themes within a mass of documents. Users are now able to browse top-down the totality of the documents, examine related documents jointly, and discover unsuspected but valuable documents and relationships."[9]

The common phrase "outside the box" graphically captures the basic point I want to make. If "the box" refers to the preestablished categories of a classificatory scheme, then to think "outside the box" means precisely to escape those categories. The indexing quality of open-ended automated searching aids and abets such an escape.

Chapter 8

The Automated Mode in Practice

A basic thesis of this book is that the automated mode of information management changes people's habits of getting and using information. These changing habits encourage open-mindedness and imaginative thinking by loosening the rigidities of culture, thus helping to alleviate the contradictions and compartmentalizations that I have characterized as the trouble with culture. An obvious example of this trend is how the Internet has transformed and democratized communication. Innumerable forums, discussion groups, newsgroups, chat rooms, and other outlets enable anyone to disseminate views on any topic to an indefinitely large audience, some of whom may respond in ongoing discussions. A particularly interesting resource for those seeking information is Wikipedia, the free encyclopedia (http://www.wikipedia.org). It consists of articles on hundreds of thousands of topics in English, German, French, Japanese, Polish, Italian, Swedish, Dutch, Portuguese, and Spanish, ranging from nearly 800,000 in English to over 70,000 in Spanish. Wikipedia's distinctive feature is that anyone can instantly and easily expand or modify any existing article or add new ones, with no membership requirement or vetting of qualifications. While this arrangement's vulnerability to inadvertent or intentional inaccuracy is obvious, the managers, contributors, and users of Wikipedia clearly think this is outweighed by the advantages of a place that accumulates, organizes, and makes readily available the knowledge of literally anyone about anything. It is a kind of ultimate in acceptance and open-mindedness; in short, the democratization or even the anarchy of knowledge: the information that anyone chooses to provide is automatically incorporated into the encyclopedia and remains there until someone else, anyone else, decides to change it. Wikipedia is actually very useful for relatively casual inquiries, although one is well advised to consult other sources to verify important information found there. In any event, the enterprise unquestionably does loosen traditional rigidities governing the dissemination of information.

The preceding chapter made an in-principle argument for how changes in habits of acquiring and using information are brought about by automation's primary reliance on indexing rather than classification. While I fully expect these developments to gain momentum with the continuing advance of automation, this is not just a prognostication of the future. The effects that I am talking about are visible here and now. This chapter describes what some of them are. We will begin by bringing up to date our earlier discussion of techniques for organizing and accessing legal information.

AUTOMATION AND THE LAW

The chronic problem facing a system of common law is that the wheels of justice never stop grinding, and the inexorable accumulation of published cases becomes increasingly difficult for lawyers to control. The West key number system and other coping techniques alleviated the situation for several decades, but by the early 1960s American lawyers were again finding that the amount of information they confronted was getting out of hand. In the mid-1960s, the Ohio State Bar Association formed a group to explore whether computers might help. It learned of a promising system originally designed to help the air force manage its huge files of procurement contracts. The Ohio Bar reached an agreement with its developers to modify the system to suit its needs. After a shaky start, Mead Data Central Corporation introduced the computerized legal research service LEXIS for nationwide marketing in 1973. The West Publishing Company, accustomed for decades to dominance in the legal publishing market, came out with the competitor WESTLAW in 1975. Initially clumsy, by 1983 or 1984, WESTLAW had become an automated research service equal in power to LEXIS (Harrington 1984–1985:543, 547–54).

LEXIS and WESTLAW place full texts of case law, legal treatises, encyclopedias, and law journals on CD-ROM and online databases, where they may be electronically searched by keyword. The impact on legal research has been immense. Manual research using "the books" was made obsolete as it became possible to do in minutes what had previously required hours of tedious work. Hyperlinks allow attorneys searching for a favorable precedent instantly to move from one opinion to another as they review cases similar to the one on which they are working. Hyperlinked footnotes in law review articles enable readers to go directly to other relevant works. The change is more fundamental than just doing the same kind of things as before, only faster. For one thing, the ease of following hyperlinks certainly results in lawyers actually consulting more cited cases and publications than they would have done when it required finding the relevant volumes in the library. In general, the transformation of how information is located has important consequences for how that information is used and by what means.

The law looks different depending on how it is researched (Berring 1986:29, 33). Nonautomated tools such as encyclopedias and treatises rely heavily on classification, while the West key number system is essentially a classified index. Much as other encyclopedias and library cataloging systems, they organize the law in a hierarchical system of categories that also serves as a device for finding legal information. As discussed in chapter 5, those who use this system come to assume that their categories reflect the actual structure of the law. This attitude is conducive to legal positivism, which holds that human laws exist in their own right, in the same way that laws of nature do. Calvin Coolidge expressed it most succinctly: "Men do not make laws. But they do discover them" (quoted in Schwartz 1993:460). That is, the categories of the taxonomic schemes for classifying legal information have been reified into principles thought to exist in their own right. It follows that the law, properly understood as emanating from independently existing principles, contains the final, absolute truth about the proper conduct of human affairs. In common law, Robert Berring holds, the positivist assumption is widespread that the truth is out there, and with proper research one can discover what it is (Berring 1994:17).[1]

In contrast, lawyers who regularly use LEXIS and WESTLAW routinely design highly customized searches that pinpoint and juxtapose information in ways that would be impossible with the West key number system or any other classified index. Roberta Shaffer stressed this point when asked what appealed to her about computerized legal research. "Being liberated," she replied. "Having the choice between looking at something using someone else's taxonomy . . . versus letting your own mind create the taxonomies. With the books, you don't have the freedom to think of it the way *you* think of it. You're constrained by how somebody else chose to present it" (quoted in Halvorson 2000:114–15, emphasis in original). Legal research of any sort, be it in case law, regulatory law, or the academic literature, is being weaned away from the hierarchical categories embedded in the traditional research tools. As a result, lawyers are coming to think of the law as a collection of facts and principles that can be assembled, disassembled (even dissembled), and reassembled in a variety of ways for different purposes (Bintliff 1996:345–46). This could call into question the notion that the law actually *has* an intrinsic, hierarchical organization, and that would signal a basic change in the perception of legal knowledge and of the law itself (Katsh 1989:221–22).

This perspective is compatible with the anti-positivist philosophies of legal realism (Berring 1986:56) and critical legal studies—variations on the theme that the application of the law is more subject to judicial biases and the hegemony of entrenched political and economic interests than abstract principles of justice.[2] I say that automated research techniques are compatible with these views, not their cause, for, as a product of the 1920s and 1930s, legal realism predates automated research techniques, while critical legal studies hale from the 1980s. Important differences separate them, the realists being more pragmatic and the "crits" more radical and ideological (Hasnas 1995:95–105, 107–108). Without going deeper into the complex question of their relationship, it is fair to say that both realists and crits reject the positivist view of the law as a perfectly consistent, independently existing system of principles discoverable by scientific techniques (see Hasnas 1995:85). Among the things the crits criticize are legal categories, which obscure the uniqueness of cases, lead jurists to treat unequal situations as equal, and promulgate a veneer of organization that hides an underlying incoherency and indeterminacy of legal doctrine. Automated research techniques do not require a practitioner to espouse the crits' view, but the absence of preestablished categories in those techniques is obviously compatible with it.

Crits also take a dim view of the application of precedent. Instead of searching first for precedent and being guided by it, they argue that judges decide according to their economic, social, and political biases and then seek out precedent to justify the conclusions they have already reached (Barkan 1987:629–30).[3] Again, automated research techniques do not force one to this view, but they can easily be called upon for support by those who affirm it. If one thinks that judges are prone to unearth precedent to support their foregone conclusions, then it is easy to point out that they are much aided in this endeavor by the ease of finding large numbers of cases electronically. Moreover, automation makes it easier for canny litigators to assemble and study previous decisions by the judges before whom they will appear, so that they may craft arguments to appeal to their biases (Berring 1986:56).

Automation may have an effect on the hallowed principle of precedent. When everyone utilized the West key number system and other preautomated research techniques, opposing attorneys would tend to develop their arguments on the basis of the same cases, nearly all of which were familiar to judges and experts in that field of law (Bintliff 1996:343–44). Keyword searches with LEXIS and WESTLAW produce different results, depending on precisely how searchers formulate their queries. This may lead different attorneys working on the same issue to different and occasionally unfamiliar cases that they may cite as precedent for the case at hand. Opinions differ as to exactly what the impact of this will be. For Berring, it has the potential to burst the bonds of conservatism and generate a dynamic that will breathe new life into the common law, as opposing attorneys base their arguments on different cases, and judges will be forced to take novel information into account as they formulate their opinions (Berring 1986:56, 1994:28–30, see also Katsh 1989:20; for a contrary opinion, see Bintliff 1996:349–50). Katsh is less sanguine: "The main threat to precedent today is that the lawyer who is searching for relevant cases now has more and more cases to choose from and can obtain such cases more and more quickly. The effect of this is to change the nature of legal argument and to diminish the authority of prior cases" (1989:45).

Interestingly, however, if automation weakens precedent in one way, then it has enabled a new version of precedent to develop in another. Automation's enhanced storage capabilities and ease of access have led many large law firms to establish internal databases consisting of the memos their attorneys make regarding the cases that they have contemplated taking. When deciding whether to take new cases and planning how to proceed with them, members consult the database to learn how the firm evaluated similar cases in the past. Attorneys and librarians I interviewed from large firms stressed that one of the benefits of this is economic, for reviewing research that the firm has already done is faster than researching an issue from scratch, and this translates into lower bills to clients. In essence, this practice perpetuates the traditional common law reliance on *stare decisis* (that previous judgments should be followed in deciding later cases), now transferred, however, to the plane of the individual law firm.

A number of analysts regard the growing role of the automated mode of information management in legal research with a jaundiced eye. They fear that it fosters bad law, as lawyers not skilled in the technique of keyword searching formulate their queries poorly and miss the cases and other information most germane to their purposes, or develop weak and inappropriate arguments on the basis of the first few cases they locate. Other attorneys may overemphasize the role of artificial intelligence, uncritically amassing staggering numbers of precedents and literature citations and thinking that their job ends there. They fail to apply their human intelligence sufficiently at the point where it is indispensable: the development of thoughtful arguments based on careful application of facts and legal principles (Lien 1998:88–89; Krause 1993:576; Selya 1994:408; Munday 1983; Bintliff 1996).

While it is not surprising that the power of automated research techniques may lull some attorneys into complacency or reveal their shortcomings, this is by no means the inevitable result. It is simply the risk that accompanies automation's liberation of human intelligence from canned categories and putting it on its own to do what it does best: seek meaning and develop interpretations and analyses. That applies to everything we have discussed about automated legal research. Whether the attorney is combing case law in search of precedent, scouring books and articles for support in developing an argument for litigation, negotiation, or publication, or reviewing notes taken by firm colleagues in similar situations to determine how to proceed with a case, the indexing technique of artificial intelligence presents human intelligence with less categorized, more diverse information to evaluate and analyze than preautomated methods, with their reliance on classification, ever did. People must use their own devices to determine, among the results of a keyword search, what is relevant and what is not, and to interpret the meaning of what they have found. Of course, some people do this better than others, and a few fail at it miserably. But the crucial point is that with the introduction of artificial intelligence in legal research, human intelligence has more latitude than before. This encourages flexibility and creativity rather than uniformity of thought (see Bolter 1991:22; DiMarco 1997).

The discussion in chapter 5 of the law before automation noted that the law, as a body of knowledge, a program of training, a body of practices, and a profession, was insulated from the rest of the university and society. This is now changing, and an important contributing factor to the shift is the automation of information. This is particularly clear on the academic side of the law. According to Bernard Schwartz (1993:566), "As this century draws to a close, the cutting edge of jurisprudence is in the academy rather than the forum. It is the 'academic scribbler,' more than the judge, who is setting the themes for the developing law." While this is probably not a universal opinion, the automation of information is making an important contribution to the development of academic law. For one thing, there is a great deal more "academic scribbling" going on now than there was thirty years ago. Professor Albert Brecht, head of the University of Southern California Law Library, emphasized in an interview that beginning in the 1970s, a major tilt toward research and publication occurred among law school faculty. This trend has continued to increase ever since, and he is convinced that an important impetus for it is automation.

Automation opens the door to new kinds of academic analysis. A greater empirical emphasis is visible in the work of legal scholars, as automation makes it easier to gather data (Mary Zulack, personal communication). For example, in their discussion of indeterminate doctrines for judicial review of administrative decisions, Shapiro and Levy (1995:1067) utilized computer searches to analyze citation patterns in fifty-six Supreme Court cases and 118 circuit court cases. Prior to automation, such a question would more likely have been addressed with a doctrinal analysis relying on a few cases.

Another major factor is the Internet, which carries vast amounts of information on virtually every topic. A faculty member with research specialization in administrative law told me that the availability of regulations and other information from state and federal agencies on the Internet has made the materials he consults much easier to access. Formerly it was often necessary to travel to Washington to visit the agency itself and have the physical documents brought out. Now administrative agencies have Web sites, their policy documents are online, and they can be retrieved immediately from virtually anywhere. He regularly consults the *Federal Register*, a very large body of information that is issued electronically every day. He finds the capacity to define his own searches in the *Register* by keywords a great improvement over reliance on prefabricated index categories. Another facilitator to his research is "push technology," whereby he can leave his keyword search strategy in the system and whenever something appears in the *Register* that suits that strategy he is automatically notified by e-mail.

Evidence of increased and more eclectic research activity by academic lawyers is especially visible in recent developments in the world of law journals. Many law faculty members now partner in research and writing with scholars from other fields (Kissam 1986:297–99, 318–19). And law journals themselves have changed. Twenty-five years ago most law schools published just one or two journals: its law review and perhaps one other, typically focused on a specific area of the law. The growth of the profession and an increased emphasis on research and publication in academic law in recent years have produced a veritable flood of new journals, with many law schools now publishing several. For example, in 1977, a sample of sixteen law schools from different geographical regions and ranked tiers published twenty-eight journals between them, most of them standard law reviews.[4] As of 2002, those same schools published a total of seventy-seven journals. The increasingly leaky boundary between the law and other fields of scholarship is evident from the fact that many of the new journals are explicitly interdisciplinary in focus, such as the *Ecology Law Quarterly, Texas Hispanic Journal of Law and Policy, Journal of Southern Legal History, Southern California Interdisciplinary Law Journal,* and *Law and Sexuality.*

Equally to the point, law schools increasingly offer joint programs with departments in the arts and sciences, such as economics, political science, history, sociology, public administration, and many others. In 1977, fourteen[5] of those same sixteen law schools offered a total number of twenty-nine formal interdisciplinary programs leading to a law degree, plus a master's degree in another discipline. By 2002, the number of interdisciplinary programs had more than doubled to seventy. And law schools also are bringing other disciplines within their own precincts. Between 1977 and 2002, the percentage of regular faculty holding doctoral degrees in both law and another discipline nearly tripled, from 5% to 13%, and there are even some members on law faculties with PhDs in other disciplines and no law degree (see Hanson 2002:589–92).

All of this evidence points unmistakably to the conclusion that the boundary between academic law and other scholarly disciplines has become more permeable in recent years. One reason for this, suggested by Richard Posner, is that by the 1950s, the law had become rather cut and dried, and academic lawyers were becoming restless to do something new and different. Exploring the relation between the law and other disciplines breathed new vitality into legal scholarship (Posner 1987:772–73).

Another reason may relate to publishers' commercial interests. These continue to have an influence on the dissemination of legal information today, just as they did when John West was building his publishing empire a century ago. Now, however, they may be a contributing factor to lessening the law's isolation. The West Publishing Company, with its automated system WESTLAW, has recently been acquired by Thomson, which publishes in many areas in addition to law. Schauer and Wise hypothesize "that the very boundary between law and nonlaw that the previously law-specific West Publishing Company had a strong interest in protecting is a boundary that Thomson, which now owns West, has an equally strong interest in tearing down. If lawyers and judges could be encouraged to become consumers of Thomson's nonlaw products, for example, and if Thomson's nonlaw customers could be encouraged to become consumers of Thomson's newly acquired law products, the most obvious winner appears to be Thomson itself" (Schauer and Wise 2000:511–12). A similar argument could be made for Mead Data Central, publisher of LEXIS-NEXIS, which has been acquired by Reed-Elsevier, a firm that is also active in publishing nonlegal materials (Schauer and Wise 1997:1107).

I suggest that a more important reason than either of these is the development of automated research tools. As Vreeland and Dempsey point out: "Technology feeds the trend toward interdisciplinary studies, as the electronic revolution blurs traditional disciplinary boundaries. . . . The apparent proximity that online systems create makes it more difficult to justify turning a blind eye to 'outside' materials" (1996:473–74). Both LEXIS and WESTLAW began as specifically legal databases available by subscription only to members of the legal profession, but their influence has widened as LEXIS was joined by a companion family of databases, NEXIS, that contained information from newspapers and many other nonlegal sources. Recently, a new version of LEXIS-NEXIS, Academic Universe, has become available via many university libraries. Although watered down in legal matters when compared to LEXIS, it adds databases devoted to news, business, medicine, congressional information, statistics of all sorts, and general reference. Add to this the many electronic resources that increasingly feature full text of works in the humanities and social sciences and it becomes obvious that legal scholars can now access with the click of a mouse a great deal of information from diverse fields that previously would have required them to make time-consuming trips to other campus libraries.

Although I have dwelt on the growing tendency of legal scholars to look outside the law, in reality traffic in the opposite direction is probably even heavier. The law is a rich source of theory and data for many issues of interest to scholars in the social sciences and humanities, such as the ethics of medicine and business, governmental policy and practice at every level, race and gender relations, and the study you are now reading. The Law and Society Association is a confluence of scholars with interests in the law from many different disciplines. Formal associations devoted to legal studies have been established within the disciplines of anthropology, sociology, psychology, political science, and history. Undergraduate programs in law and society are on the rise. Automation has given these trends added impetus. The automated mode of information management was incorporated earlier and has proceeded further in law than in other disciplines. Judicial opinions, legal periodicals, treatises, and other important information sources have been available for over two decades through LEXIS and WESTLAW, while full-text journal articles and books in the humanities and social sciences began coming online considerably later. The ready accessibility of legal information as a rich source of data for a variety of issues has been a strong enticement for non-lawyers to extend their research into the law.

Interdisciplinary movements also are visible in the practice of law. In the world of large law firms, this has primarily taken the form of linking specialties within the law rather than lawyers with outsiders. Firms are often organized into practice groups, many of which combine attorneys with complementary skills. Some practice groups are permanent, such as employment law, international trade, mergers and acquisitions, and other standard practice areas. Others form to deal with specific issues, a good example being the Y2K practice groups that sprang up in many firms in the late 1990s. These brought together attorneys with a variety of specializations (technology, warranty liability, contracts, insurance) to address the anticipated crisis associated with computer date changes in 2000. Firm intranets and other automated procedures enable members of practice groups to remain in close communication, even when they are located in different cities.

In the courts, judges today are citing more nonlegal sources in their opinions than previously. Schauer and Wise (2000) examined all citations in U.S. Supreme Court opinions at five-year intervals, from 1960 to 1990, and then for each year from 1990 to 1998. While the trajectory is by no means smooth, they found a distinct increase in the proportion of citations to nonlegal material. Samplings from the Supreme Court of New Jersey and other courts showed a similar pattern. The notion that nonlegal information helps develop the best cases and opinions is scarcely new (Barkan 1990:33–35). Louis Brandeis relied heavily on social scientific data in the 1907 case *Muller v. Oregon,* setting a precedent famous and influential enough that briefs using information drawn from outside sources have become common and are regularly called "Brandeis briefs." Still, automated information technology has significantly boosted the practice. Schauer and Wise center their analysis on the ease of electronic searching. "In previously barely imagined ways the universe of nonlegal information is now easily and cheaply available to lawyers, judges, and other legal decision makers. What once would have required a two-hour journey now requires only the click of a mouse, and this may well provide the most persuasive explanation of the phenomenon we have identified" (Schauer and Wise 2000:513).

The Internet also breaches the boundary between the law and the rest of society, as laypersons use it to gain familiarity with legal matters. One upshot of this is that many distaff visions of what the law is or should be are now promulgated by a wide variety of groups, including supremacists of one sort or another, militias, survivalists, and religious sects. Another is that individuals who face a legal issue often turn to the Internet to learn more about their situation, and they may become quite knowledgeable in that particular area of the law. Depending on how well they contextualize that knowledge and realize their limitations, this can either help or hinder their attorneys. More knowledgeable clients also pose a threat to attorneys of marginal competence. A similar situation notoriously exists in medicine, where patients accumulate information about their diagnosed conditions on the Internet and sometimes secondguess their physicians accordingly.

SCHOLARLY RESEARCH AND EDUCATION

Law is just one example of a general trend toward greater openness that stems in part from automation. Another is the academy. The circumstance leading to the formation of academic disciplines was that knowledge stored in artificial memory exponentially increased with the passage of time and with inventions such as printing. As it became more and more evident that the Renaissance Man could not survive long after the Renaissance, and that no individual could hope to control all knowledge, people specialized in one or another segment of it. Recorded information continues to multiply today, more prolifically than ever, as the number of scholars who produce it is larger, and electronic databases make it possible to store and promulgate massive amounts of information more easily, more rapidly, and more compactly than was ever possible with written or printed text. It has been estimated that the total bulk of information doubles every ten to fifteen years (Tehranian 1996:442). It might be expected that this, an "appalling glut" in its own right, would make specialization even narrower and more pronounced. But in fact, something quite different has happened.

With characteristic prescience, forty years ago Marshall McLuhan recognized a new dimension. After discussing the growth of specialization, he wrote: "At the extreme of speeded-up movement, however, specialism of space and subject disappears once more. . . . Centuries of specialist stress in pedagogy and in the arrangement of data now end with the instantaneous retrieval of information made possible by electricity" (McLuhan 1994 [1964]:346). Previously the taxonomic classification of scholarly specializations served to sequester knowledge and learning into separate compartments. But, as is more evident in our time than it was in McLuhan's, automated information retrieval techniques based on indexing instantly bring together information on any topic from a variety of specialized fields. This juxtaposition of information makes the hitherto unrecognized relevance of research on a topic in one field apparent for work being done in another. Possibilities for new insights derived from sharing findings and methods and for future collaboration leap into view. The work of each researcher may still be specialized, in some cases more than ever, but automated information retrieval enables the researcher to become aware of what the others are doing. The researcher perceives common ground, upon which the differences between the contributions of scholars from different fields become recognized as complementary rather than compartmentalized. Disciplinary separation gives way to interdisciplinary cooperation.

I had a research assistant undertake two quantitative investigations in an effort to gather empirical evidence pertaining to the proposition that automation has encouraged interdisciplinary research and scholarship. The first compared scholarly journals in the humanities and social sciences founded in 1970, before automated information management had emerged in those scholarly fields, with those founded in 1995, when it had become well established. If automation encourages interdisciplinary scholarship, then a greater percentage of new journals founded in 1995 should be interdisciplinary than those founded in 1970. The findings supported this hypothesis, for 31% of the 211 new journals founded in 1995 are interdisciplinary, as opposed to 21% of the 166 journals founded in 1970.

The second investigation compared bibliographic citations in scholarly journal articles in 1975–1976 with those in 2000–2001. Specifically, all citations in the first article in the second issue of ten leading American humanities and social science journals[6] for each of those years were classed as being clearly within the same discipline as the journal, interdisciplinary, or unable to judge. We expected that more citations would be interdisciplinary in the later period, when automated research techniques made it much easier to access sources from different disciplines than in the earlier period. Again, the results bore out the hypothesis, although less strongly than in the first study. Interdisciplinary citations increased from 18% in 1975–1976 to 21% in 2000–2001.

Although the instantaneous access to information made possible by the automated mode of information management plays a pivotal part, it is not the only factor contributing to the breakdown of disciplinary isolation. Nor is it the first. Taxonomic classification of the disciplines is the foundation of their compartmentalization, and several forces were undermining it well before automation came on the scene. The first cracks in taxonomic classification appeared in the seventeenth century as one legacy of the scientific revolution. With Newton, physical science abandoned the taxonomic approach in favor of an atomistic-mechanistic perspective. That is, scientists began to turn their attention to parts and to ask how they combine to form various wholes. This new paradigm differed radically from the taxonomic one. Instead of naming and organizing things hierarchically according to their observable qualities, the focus turned to the operation of unseen particles governed by invariable laws, inferred from quantitative measurements and expressed mathematically (see Slaughter 1982:190–96). A similar development is now occurring in molecular biology, as the burgeoning interest in genetics manifests the same shift from a taxonomic approach to an atomistic-mechanical one. Certainly genetics can be used for taxonomic purposes such as measuring the propinquity between certain populations and species, but there is greater interest in identifying how particular genes contribute to the makeup and functioning of organisms. In themselves, these developments do not necessarily lead away from disciplinary specialization, but they do weaken taxonomy, which is one of the pillars upon which the disciplines rest.

Again, the taxonomic classification of the sciences, which had been a major subject of interest through the nineteenth century, dwindled in the twentieth century (Dolby 1979:167). One reason for this was that, under the influence of the Vienna School, philosophers of science were becoming more interested in the common methodology that unites the different sciences than in the subject matters that distinguish them (ibid., p. 188). Another is that the practice of science itself was changing. Nineteenth-century science justified itself mainly as adding to knowledge, filling in our understanding of the world. This was conducted in the context of the various disciplines, each of which had carved out a part of the world as its domain for investigation. In the twentieth century, research turned more toward practical applications in war and industry (pp. 187–88) and to focused questions in basic research. Science shifted from discipline orientation toward problem orientation, and many problems do not fall neatly within the confines of any one discipline.

The ascendance of problem-oriented, interdisciplinary research is much in evidence today. For example, the National Science Foundation influences the overall course of scientific research in the United States by allocating a portion of its funding resources to certain areas it designates as priorities. A recent one is the Human and Social Dynamics priority area. The program description reads, in part, "Revolutionary technologies and ideas that are the product of human minds have created a more closely linked world, within which there is almost instantaneous transmission of information that feeds a global economy. But it is also a world of change, uncertainty, and disruption that leaves many uncertain how to respond. . . . Scientific understanding of the dynamics of mental processes, individual behavior, and social activity increasingly requires partnerships that span the different science, engineering, and education communities."[7] Because contemporary research initiatives such as this are concerned with specific questions to be answered or problems to be solved instead of furthering knowledge in the traditional domains of the disciplines, they tend to be, as this one emphatically is, interdisciplinary in nature. Private enterprises such as pharmaceutical and aeronautic companies and other federal agencies that support scientific research—the Department of Defense, the Department of Energy, the National Institutes of Health—are even more directive in defining the particular applications of scientific research that they are willing to fund, many of which also involve interdisciplinary teamwork.

The trend toward interdisciplinary, problem-oriented research involves the same shift in mind-set that we have already identified in the decline of classifying and the growth of indexing. It is a change in how the relation between wholes and parts is conceptualized. Discipline-oriented research is part of the classificatory worldview that begins with a predetermined whole (the sector of reality reserved to that discipline or subdiscipline) within which the place of any part is already established, or, for newly encountered parts, at least strongly anticipated. The typical research activity in this paradigm is to try to demonstrate how each part does in fact fit the whole in the expected way, or, if it does not, to explain why not.

Problem-oriented, interdisciplinary research, on the other hand, manifests the worldview we have identified with indexing. It operates in an ad hoc manner, open to a wide range of information from diverse sources. It lacks preconceived notions about what the relevant whole is, what the component parts are, and how they fit together to form it. The research process is open-ended. It consists of sifting through a wide range of data for material that seems relevant (recognizing that what is or is not relevant may change as the investigation proceeds) and building a conclusion on the basis of facts and concepts that may never have been combined in that way before.

Problem-oriented, interdisciplinary research takes at least two distinguishable forms. On the one hand, some scholars remain closely tethered to their particular specializations, but they collaborate with specialists in other fields, as in multidisciplinary scientific research projects. Often such teams dissolve when the project is finished, and new teams form around other projects. Individuals may belong to a sequence of them over several years. In these cases, the interdisciplinary quality of research characterizes the collaborating team as a whole but not necessarily its individual members.

On the other hand, individual scholars often cross disciplinary lines as they address particular projects. Those dealing with contemporary questions of ethics, for example, draw not only upon traditional ethics in philosophy but also, depending on the particular issue they are addressing, on recent developments in medicine and assisted reproduction, genetics, business practices, globalization, and so forth. A seminal work in the interdisciplinary movement of cultural studies was the 1968 book *Lawrence and Oppenheimer,* by Nuel Pharr Davis. In researching and writing the book, which is something of a cultural history of the making of the atomic bomb, English professor Davis acquired a professional-level competence in physics (Nelson and Gaonkar 1996:1–3). Davis's odyssey was unusual for the 1960s, but the career trajectories of many scholars today manifest a similar pattern. Instead of career-long specialization in Polynesian ethnology or Victorian poetry, scholars increasingly cross borders between conventional specializations as they design and pursue new research or practice problems.

Whether done in teams or individually, problem-oriented, interdisciplinary research generates a new fluidity in scholars' social relations just as it does in their worldview. Affiliations to traditional fields of study and the connections scholars establish among themselves are loosened. Traditionally they formed themselves into relatively long-term, stable groups or interpretive communities defined by specialization. These often are associations with formal names, officers, annual meetings, journals, and so forth. Examples are the Pacific Art Association, the Society for Medical Anthropology, the Milton Society of America, the Royal Society of Chemistry, the American Association of Physicists in Medicine, and so on. Such organizations continue to flourish today. Now, however, those who address a sequence of different issues or problems in their careers find themselves attending and presenting papers at meetings of an eclectic set of professional organizations and establishing short-term associations with bodies of literature and other professionals most helpful to their current projects, to be followed later by other organizations, literatures, and scholars pertinent to their subsequent research interests.

All of these changes in the pattern of scholarly research owe much to the ready access to information on any topic enabled by the automated mode of information management. Researchers can easily learn about what people in other fields have been doing on problems related to their own. That piques their interest, as well as their sense of scholarly responsibility to take account of others' work that has been done on their topic of research. And when they do take account of it, not uncommonly the result is to change and broaden their own paths of research and ultimate conclusions. What Ethan Katsh said with reference to the law is equally apt for scholars in other disciplines: "Speed and convenience may be the attraction for new computer users and the justification for purchasing hardware and software, but most users at some point find themselves using information differently, possessing information that they would not have had previously, asking questions they might not have asked previously and working with people they might not have had contact with before" (Katsh 1993:443).

The disciplines have been sites of education as well as research, and the interdisciplinary turn is also visible there. In chapter 4 I discussed how individuals who are trained and operate within the context of an established discipline are apt to be mentally conditioned by that discipline. That is, the way such persons view the world—their expectations about what is likely to be connected with or explained by what—is conditioned by the assumptions built into their disciplinary education. It is an application of what Foucault (1977) called the disciplinary technology of power. That is essentially a method of social control based on a program of training that breaks down desired behaviors into sets of component parts and requires trainees to repeat each part until its perfect reproduction becomes almost unconsciously habitual. The disciplinary technology conditions people to the extent that power can be wielded over them with minimal heavy enforcement. The phrase is doubly apt in this context, because individuals who are educated under the regime of the scholarly disciplines are disciplined by years of indoctrination in the assumptions, expectations, standard questions, and methods for answering them associated with each field (Usher, Bryant, and Johnston 1997:83, 89). As with other applications of disciplinary power, this one is subtle enough that people generally do not realize what is taking place.

Although automation is not exclusively responsible for the trend away from disciplinary isolation, it has become a contributing factor to the liberation of people from the discipline of the disciplines. The open-ended, ad hoc conditions brought about by increased emphasis on indexing in the automated mode of information management bypass the established, predefined, discipline-based conditions of the oral and textual modes, with their reliance on classifying. This frees thought to move in new directions and explore previously unrecognized possibilities.

The growth of interdisciplinary programs in the universities was stimulated in part by the tendency toward multidisciplinary, problem-oriented research. Scholars, thinking that what they teach ought to be more in line with what they do as researchers, began to design curricula and degree programs that spilled over the borders between different disciplines as traditionally defined. Students, for their part, began to seek training that reflected their personal interests. In contrast to the "subject-oriented" learning that Patricia Cranton associated with fixed disciplines (as discussed in chapter 4), Cranton identifies two other forms of learning: "consumer oriented" and "emancipatory" (1994:10–19). In the first and especially the second of these, learners take more initiative in the educational process, selecting what they will study on the basis of their particular needs and interests. The result of such rethinking on the parts of both teachers and students is the institutionalization of interdisciplinary studies. Programs in human development combine biology with psychology and other social sciences. Natural, biological, and social sciences all figure in programs in ecology, some of which also incorporate history and literature. Programs in cultural studies, women's studies, gay and lesbian studies, and peace and conflict studies draw upon history, literature, philosophy, and several of the social sciences in various combinations. In 2004, Princeton University inaugurated a new freshman and sophomore science curriculum designed to teach chemistry, physics, biology, and computation in an integrated fashion over four semesters. The sequence features a "just-in-time" approach that, in common with manufacturing procedures that provide materials only when they are needed, introduces concepts and methods at the moment they will be used to address specific questions rather than presenting them at the beginning with the assurance that they will come in handy later.

Interdisciplinary curricula are relatively recent; over 80% of them were established after 1971 (Klein 1990:180). Geographic area studies were among the first interdisciplinary programs to appear in American universities. Today, every large university and many small ones have formal programs in several areas, such as American studies, East Asian studies, South Asian studies, African studies, Middle Eastern studies, Slavic studies, Latin American studies, and so on. These bring together faculty scholars from virtually all of the disciplines in the humanities and social sciences. At the dawn of the 1960s, I myself majored in one of the first of these area programs, Princeton's Special Program in European Civilization.[8] Its founder, Ira Wade, articulated the highly interdisciplinary vision that still guides virtually all such programs (and my own career as an anthropologist): "to penetrate another civilization through its language, its history, its arts and letters, its manners and customs." The idea is that life as it actually is lived is not segmented into disciplines. Therefore, studying it through the lens of any one traditional discipline misses a full understanding of a particular region, while approaching it simultaneously through several disciplines enhances it.

The emphasis on interdisciplinary studies has even produced efforts to organize entire universities on that basis. These include the University of Wisconsin at Green Bay, Tromso University in Norway, Roskilde Institute in Copenhagen, the Universty of Tsukuba in Japan, Griffith University in Australia, and Sussex, East Anglia, and the Open Universities in Britain (Klein 1990:156–63). St. John's College bases its four-year curriculum of all required courses on a roughly chronological survey of the great books of Western Civilization, while Alaska Pacific University for a time followed a highly integrated four-year interdisciplinary core curriculum based on four environments: natural environment (freshmen), social environment (sophomores), individual environment (juniors), and spiritual environment (seniors) (p. 167).[9]

The decline of discipline-oriented research and education parallels the decline of classification discussed in chapters 6 and 7. Disciplinary organization and classifying both represent a worldview born of the oral and textual modes of information management, a worldview that assumes a reality divided into preestablished categories. It is a worldview that sets for knowledge seekers the task of fitting new information into one or another of those categories, and to deal with it according to the methods appropriate to that category. On the other hand, interdisciplinary learning and research join indexing—especially automated indexing—in a worldview that is particularly compatible with thinking that combines artificial and human intelligence. It is a worldview that thrives on contingency, that treats each issue or problem as potentially pertaining to a wide range of relevant information drawn from a variety of sources. The automated mode of information management, and particularly its accent on indexing, is conducive to this kind of worldview because, on the one hand, it is not adept at recognizing how particular bits of information might fit into larger categories at various hierarchical levels of generalization, and also because, on the other hand, it is extremely proficient at rapidly finding matches for bits of information in very large databases of any and all subject matters. This is not only congenial to human intelligence, but it actually amplifies it, because it throws up unanticipated combinations of information upon which the human mind can then exercise its peculiar powers of interpretation. This is more likely to occur in interdisciplinary learning and research than it is when those activities are bound by the disciplines. Knowledge seekers and knowledge itself have been liberated from assumptions that assign a place for everything in advance. Boundaries between so-called disciplines lose relevance as students seek to broaden their understanding by approaching the subject matter from several different angles and as the particular problem before a researcher takes center stage and what is important to it becomes a matter of discovery. Most of the truly insightful works of our time, such as Marshall McLuhan's (1994 [1964]) *Understanding Media* and Michel Foucault's (1977) *Discipline and Punish,* emerge from scholarship that is not easily classified within any conventionally defined discipline.

BUSINESS AND MANUFACTURING

Parallel developments are visible in many business and manufacturing enterprises, where ad hoc teams that form specifically to accomplish certain tasks are becoming common. The head of an Australian consulting firm said, "Consulting is a bit like film production units—they come together and do the job and then disband" (Trinca 2004). Automation has enabled many such teams to be "virtual," with members located in many different places, who interact via e-mail and other kinds of electronic communication (Coleman 1997; Maznevski and Chudoba 2000). So pervasive is this trend that the Gartner Group forecasted in 2002 that by 2005, 80% of all global knowledge work would be delivered by virtual project teams "that work together but are physically apart. Their activities are often time-bound—they come together to accomplish a specific task and when their objective is met, they disband, with members joining other newly forming project teams" (Kaplan 2002:3).

A number of on-the-fly responses have been designed to maximize efficiency and respond to consumer wants with maximum speed. Kawasaki plants use "a 'just-in-time' supply method which eliminates expensive warehousing and over-ordering of parts. . . . For instance, certain parts and pieces are made on special presses located right on the assembly line. This means no shortages or excess inventory on these items for more efficiency and less cost. In many cases, it also means the worker makes the part he assembles, and thus enjoys a full sense of accomplishment."[10] Again, "in the industrial districts of Italy and Germany, researchers discovered congeries of firms making apparel or ceramics that cooperated so intensely that they seemed to blur the line between market and organization. Using flexible-production methods to tailor products to rapidly fluctuating demand, these companies worked together on a routine basis, sharing workers, outsourcing to one another during times of high demand, even loaning machinery as the situation required" (DiMaggio 2001:19, citing Sabel and Zeitlin 1997).[11] All these "just-in-time" techniques rely on computer software to maximize efficiency in tracking orders, inventory, and delivery. Just-in-time production may be combined with "agile manufacturing," where automated production lines products customized to suit the needs of particular customers. "Motorola has developed an automated factory with the ability to produce physically different pagers on the same production line. At Panasonic, a combination of flexible manufacturing and just-in-time processing is being used to manufacture bicycles from combinations of a group of core parts."[12]

The organizational structure of business firms is also changing. The familiar hierarchical structure and multilevel bureaucracy that controlled all decision making and work assignments is declining in favor of more horizontal kinds of organization (Belbin 1996:vi). The impact of this is especially visible at the middle-manager-level. These managers acquire greater decision-making powers while needing to demonstrate a wider range of competencies and more initiative (Farquhar 1998; see also Ostroff 1999). As with virtual project teams, the looser form of organization features direct communication and collaboration between different units or departments, and this is greatly facilitated by e-mail, intranets, and other automated techniques.

All of these developments in business and manufacturing share the common feature of increased flexibility: to modify products according to consumer demand, to form virtual project teams, and to interact with people in different departments to address particular issues. In every case an essential enabling factor for the increased flexibility is automation, and an important result is less isolation—between different segments in the corporate structure, between offices in different localities, and even between different types of products. Here too, as in other areas we have examined, automation helps transform compartmental differences into complementary ones.

Chapter 9

The New Superorganic

Up until now, the discussion has focused on the consequences of changes that automation brings about in storing, retrieving, and applying information. This chapter[1] explores a different but related set of far-reaching consequences of automation. These have to do with transformations in the notion of who or what undertakes action, and the concept of the individual.

Before the advent of the automated mode, all information was managed in the oral and textual modes. The difference between them is that memory is human in the oral mode and artificial in the textual mode. In both of them, however, the information processor is human intelligence. Although different people often act together in groups, it is usually possible to identify the individuals who participate in the process and (although this can be quite difficult in practice) to sort out the contribution of each. In other words, the operation of human intelligence can, in principle, always be described in terms of the activities of individuals. But with the rise of the automated mode of information management, human intelligence is routinely supplemented by artificial intelligence in the conduct of a great many activities. In these circumstances, I will argue, to define the agent that manages information as the human individual is no longer a viable option. Something more complex and variable is required. Such a redefinition has serious consequences for some of social theory's basic premises about just what it is that thinks and acts. In a way different from but no less palpable than the shift from classifying to indexing, this also alleviates the trouble with culture by relaxing some of its rigid, closed categories.

First, consider the reasoning behind the coronation of the individual as the agent in social action. It is enshrined in the theoretical approach to human behavior known as methodological individualism.[2] Probably no one has stated the theory more crisply than Anthony Flew: "All social collectivities are composed of individuals, and can act only through the actions of their components. Whatever is said about any mass movement, organized collectivity, or other supposed social whole, must at some stage be related and in some way reduced to discourse about the doings, beliefs, attitudes, and dispositions of its components. Who actually did and thought what; and what led them to act and to think, as in fact they did, and not otherwise? . . . All this, once it has been sharply stated, should appear obvious and altogether beyond dispute" (Flew 1995:61–62).

Methodological individualism may be linked to the kinds of differences at the heart of the trouble with culture. The individual, based on this view, is always already compartmentalized. It is a distinct monad who may regularly associate with other persons and things but maintains through it all its separate identity. Indeed, this is a cherished quality of individual, variously described as "integrity" or "independence." But it also connotes a certain isolation, which renders individuals subject to compartmentalization from each other.

The individual of methodological individualism is also prone to contradictory difference. It belongs to a "phallogocentric" worldview (Haraway 1991:176) that thrives on distinguishing things: light from dark, male from female, good from evil. When things are distinguished, there is a tendency to oppose them (good vs. evil, light vs. dark, male vs. female), and when things are opposed, they contend, one side striving to conquer the other (good vanquishing evil, light overcoming darkness, male dominating—or, in more gentlemanly, biblical phrasing, "going before"—female). In the methodological individualist view, the individual is set apart from other individuals, things, and circumstances it encounters. By the aforementioned chain of reasoning, it may follow that the individual's distinctiveness becomes opposition to, and then contention with other individuals and things, ultimately overcoming or succumbing to them. In this way the concept of the independent, integral individual is fertile ground for contradictory difference and, as such, upholds closed culture.

However, the foundation of this concept of the individual is crumbling. Numerous reports have been bruited of late about the demise or adulteration of the autonomous individual, in the light of which it has become anything but obvious that it can any longer be taken as the sole engine of social action. One line of argument questions the historical standing of the individual as the basic unit in social life. Another holds that the development of artificial intelligence means that entities other than or in addition to human individuals now share the role of author of action. I will propose a theory of agency alternative to methodological individualism that takes this new, broader reality into account. Because a famous historical rival to methodological individualism that also aimed to extend agency beyond the individual was known as the superorganic (Kroeber 1917), I will refer to this alternative as the "new superorganic." It is not, however, just a dusted-off version of the concept as it was originally advanced long ago. It is a view of agency as consisting of multiple components, some of them human and some of them not. Moreover, it differs from human individuals in having no permanent or enduring form. It composes and recomposes itself in different configurations, each tailored specifically to the particular activity to be undertaken. No predetermined unit—the individual—undertakes action in all circumstances. Quite the reverse: particular sets of circumstances come first, and agencies form specifically to deal with them. Its contingency, fluidity, and indeterminacy set the new superorganic agency against the determinacy and permanence favored by closed culture. It is therefore a force that works quietly and subtly, but nonetheless effectively, to open culture.

DECENTERING THE INDIVIDUAL

To prepare the ground for a more fluid notion of agency, we begin with some ideas intended to dethrone the historical individual as the stable, sole author of social action. Many scholars have regarded the individual as the construct of a particular era rather than a constant through all history (Foucault 1980:117). Following Burckhardt (1954 [1860]:100–101), Erich Fromm held that the individual was born in the Renaissance. "Medieval society," he wrote, "did not deprive the individual of his freedom, because the 'individual' did not yet exist. . . . [Man] did not yet conceive of himself as an individual except through the medium of his social . . . role" (Fromm 1941:43). Louis Althusser also sees the individual as a contingent, constructed being. In his "Reply to John Lewis," Althusser argues that the engine of history for Marxism-Leninism is not "man" but the class struggle. Human nature is a variable product of particular forms of social relations; the idea of the individual as a transcendental agent struggling through history for freedom and independence is nothing more than the concoction of bourgeois ideology (Althusser 1976:46–54).

Even if of relatively recent origin, the individual may already be in the twilight of its career. In their review of steps toward postmodernist social theory, Best and Kellner stress the structuralists' and poststructuralists' increasingly radical rejection of humanistic assumptions about the autonomous subject and unchanging human nature (Best and Kellner 1991:19–20, 27). One prominent theorist imagines that this concept of the individual may be disappearing, "like a face, drawn in sand, at the edge of the sea" (Foucault 1970:387).[3]

Edward Said explains Foucault's project in language that simultaneously illuminates the grip of the individual on recent social theory and identifies some of the sources of the growing disenchantment with it: "Classical European philosophy from Descartes to Kant had supposed that an objectively stable and sovereign ego (as in 'cogito ergo sum') was both the source and basis for all knowledge. Foucault's work not only disputes this but also shows how the subject is a construction laboriously put together over time, and one very liable to be a passing historical phenomenon replaced in the modern age by transhistorical impersonal forces, like the capital of Marx or the unconscious of Freud or the will of Nietzsche" (Said 2000:16; see also Kincaid 1997:2). Elsewhere Said cites, in addition to Foucault, Lévi-Strauss, Barthes, and Lacan, as also discerning the end of the subject (Said, 1985:292–93), and one may add Deleuze and Guattari (1983) as well.[4]

The individual is in trouble in more places than just French philosophy. In Melanesia, aboriginal Australia, and elsewhere the person is defined as much by position in a network of social relations as by individual traits (Strathern and Stewart 1998; Wagner 1991; Myers 1986). The same view has been proposed for psychology by Kenneth Gergen: "We may be entering a new era of self-conception. In this era the self is redefined as no longer an essence in itself, but relational" (Gergen 1991:146). "The concept of the individual self," he continues, "ceases to be intelligible. At this point one is prepared for the new reality of relationship. Relationships make possible the concept of the self. Previous possessions of the individual self—autobiography, emotions, and morality—become possessions of relationships" (p. 170).

Psychologists and other social scientists also have questioned the autonomy of the human individual via the concept of distributed or socially shared cognition (Resnick, Levine, and Teasley 1991; Derry, DuRussel, and O'Donnell 1998; Moore and Rocklin 1998). Thus Jean Lave analyzes learning as a social rather than an individual matter (1991:64), while Edwin Hutchins meticulously demonstrates how the computational process of navigating a ship can be fully understood only in terms of teams of individuals coordinating their several activities with each other and with various technological instruments (Hutchins 1991, 1995). As Lucy Suchman put it, "Humans and artifacts are mutually constituted. . . . Agency—and associated accountabilities—reside neither in us nor in our artifacts, but in our intra-actions" (2000:9).

Yet another challenge to the centrality of the individual goes under the name actor-network theory. As developed by students of science, technology, and society, this theory attributes agency not to human individuals but to networks, finite in duration and variable in composition, defined according to the activity under analysis (Callon 1987:93, 1999:182–83; Law 1999:3–7; Latour 1987:84, 89, 1988). These actor-networks include, in addition to human beings, a wide variety of nonhuman components (Law 1991:10–11, 16–17; Star 1991:32–33). Thus the network in play in John Law's (1987) analysis of fifteenth-century Portuguese exploration includes designs of ships and the materials for constructing them, navigational devices and techniques, prevailing winds and currents, and the hospitality (or lack of it) of the West African coast in addition to Portuguese sailors.

Distributed cognition and actor-network theory are applicable at any time and place. However, only recently has it become inescapably clear that the stable, autonomous Cartesian individual is no longer tenable. What has brought about this clarity is a series of developments in technology.

For one thing, technology has breached boundaries and caused formerly distinct entities quite literally to interpenetrate and flow into each other. One example is transgenic organisms. Tomatoes containing a gene from a deep water flounder are less susceptible to freezing, a gene from the giant silk moth has been introduced into potatoes to make them more resistant to disease, and efforts are afoot to "splice carbon-based life forms to silicon-based computer systems" (Haraway 1997:230, 216). The increasingly intimate connections between humans' and nonhuman entities such as prosthetic devices and machines (especially computers), and our growing dependence on them, bring about a functionally equivalent kind of splicing that transforms us into cyborgs: new kinds of beings partly organic and partly mechanical (Haraway 1991).

Many social thinkers have acknowledged that social interaction involves entities beyond human individuals but still insist that methodological individualism is the appropriate explanatory strategy, because individuals are the control centers where decision making (conscious or not) takes place. It is of course true that no matter how elaborate the technology, the vast majority of activity today is initiated and controlled by individuals. But it is nevertheless important to recognize that with the development of artificial intelligence, certain nonhuman agents make decisions and engage in other intelligent activities. Knowledge-based or expert systems are computer programs that do the work of human experts, such as drawing up wills or diagnosing disease. Some applications can undertake a variety of tasks without the participation of any human being. Computers not only play chess against human opponents but also against other computers, as when Deep Junior won the right to meet Garry Kasparov by defeating eighteen other programs in a 2002 worldwide competition (Gray 2003). Microsoft likens its Message Queue Server to "electronic mail, except senders and receivers are application programs instead of people—and messages are data instead of electronic letters." One of its potential uses is to monitor stock in a retail outlet and send orders to the warehouse distribution center, where another computer receives the orders and issues shipping instructions, all without human input.[5]

In principle, it would be possible to analyze activities such as these in terms of the intentions and activities of the humans who programmed the software (Bolter 1991:188). However, to to do so would be intolerably time consuming, difficult, and futile (see Harris 1999:54). With CAD-CAM (computer-assisted design, computer-assisted manufacture), computers participate in making new computers. Especially with systems that learn, the line of derivation back to the original work of human programmers becomes longer, more convoluted, and harder to trace. Neural nets and genetic algorithms, for example, learn "directly from data without human intervention . . . by trawling through hundreds or thousands of past transactions" (Goonatilake 1995:5). After a certain period, such a system could develop into something quite different from its beginning. It is getting to the point where human beings are hard pressed even to understand the end product (Rawlins 1997:37).

Consider Tierra, a computer program designed by biologist Thomas Rey to simulate evolution by natural selection. Rey began with a self-replicating digital creature consisting of eighty instructions. Its progeny were designed to replicate themselves with fewer instructions, being selected by using less CPU (central processing unit)time in an environment where that is a scarce resource. Over the generations and with no further human intervention, the system produced new, more efficient creatures. Small parasitic creatures emerged that co-opted the features of larger ones. In response, some of the host creatures developed immunity to the first generation of parasites, following which new parasites capable of penetrating the hosts' defenses were replicated. Rey, the original programmer, could not predict the developments that were taking place (Turkle 1998:321). To attempt to reduce the latter stages of such a system to the intentions and decisions of the original human programmer would be devilishly difficult, as well as pointless.

THE NEW SUPERORGANIC

My conclusion from all of this is that the human individual can no longer be considered be sufficient as the unit of sociocultural action. With automation, the stable, Cartesian individual is giving way to fluid networks consisting of multiple human beings plus various nonhuman elements. We need a model that allows a way of thinking about how artificial intelligence participates in units that include but extend beyond the individual. We need an agent that is simultaneously concrete and dynamic: made of tangible stuff and yet variable in composition and duration, transcending the misleading distinction between object and event altogether. In brief, we need something superorganic that combines the fluidity of actor-networks with the concreteness of the cyborg.

A good place to start looking is Gregory Bateson's provocative insight that the agent conducting any activity should be defined to include the lines of communication essential to that activity rather than cutting across them. He instances a blind man using a stick to walk down the street. The agent in this case should not be limited to the man but rather should include all of the essential communicating components: the man, the stick, and the street. Agency, that is, is superorganic: it extends beyond the human component. Bateson's view also entails that agency be fluid, because while it clearly entails concrete components, what the components are and what they do vary according to particular activities (Bateson 1972a:459; see also Wood 1998; Hutchins 1995:291–92). Thus the agency involved when that same blind man reads a book in Braille includes the raised markings on the page but not the stick or the street. The fluidity and variablility of agency are brought out better by thinking of it verbally, as an embodied activity ("a man reading a book in Braille") rather than as a thing.

While Bateson's examples are useful for demonstrating that entities beyond the human should be included in the notion of agency, in his example of the blind man the center of intelligence or information processing is still exclusively human. White sticks, streets, and texts in Braille do not have intelligence. However, with the advent of the automated mode of information management, the information processing that governs behavior is no longer limited to human intelligence. This has serious consequences for the theoretical issue of agency. Methodological individualism serves reasonably well to explain behavior in the preautomated context, for in both the oral and textual modes the information processor is human intelligence. Although it is necessary to take into account the interactions of multiple individuals in the oral mode, information stored outside of human minds in the textual mode, and various kinds of objects and technologies in both, it is still possible to argue that evaluation, motivation, and decisions for action in both of those modes are ultimately explicable in terms of the intelligent behavior of individual human beings. But this is not true of the automated mode, where artificial rather than human intelligence evaluates information and determines action. Little if any social action is conducted exclusively in the automated mode, but it increasingly supplements the oral and textual modes. Actions that include the automated mode cannot be explained entirely in terms of the decisions and dispositions of individual human beings, and their analysis therefore requires a superorganic concept of agency that takes artificial intelligence into account. As David Hakken said, "It is necessary to recast the objects of study, to no longer draw the boundary of the field's object at the human skin but treat humans and their technologies as unitary entities. A range of anthro-techno-science concepts (such as cyborgs and Creolized Objects) can help to do this" (Hakken 1999:224; see also Downey 1995:369; Clark 2003; Selinger and Engström n.d.). While this reconfiguration may strain the tolerance of many social theorists of the present generation, it is more natural to those of the next. From their exposure to computer games and educational programs, today's children readily think of digital entities as alive, and they are comfortable with indeterminate boundaries between organism and machine (Turkle 1998).[6]

Because superorganic agencies act in combinations of human and artificial memory and human and artificial intelligence, and it is useful to sort out the role of each. Consider a student using an online catalog to find a book in a library. The agency that undertakes this task consists of at least four components: (1) the human intelligence of the student who decides to look up a particular book and knows how to manipulate the computer to do so; (2) information stored in his or her human memory regarding the author or title of the book and why it is desired; (3) artificial memory in the form of the library's database, which holds information regarding the materials it owns; and (4) artificial intelligence, consisting of what the computer hardware and software do to connect the student to information in artificial memory: processing the input about the author's name or title entered by the student into an output of call number, location, availability, and other information about the book.

Agency, as I have said, is temporary in duration and variable in composition. Imagine, for example, that after checking out the book the student telephones a friend to discuss it. Now a different agency is in play, including some but not all of the components of the first agency, along with some additional ones. Here human intelligence is represented by the information processing activities of the two people in the give and take of their conversation, and human memory contains what either knows about the contents of the book and other relevant facts and concepts. Artificial memory refers to the book itself or written notes that one or both of them may have at hand in the course of the conversation, and artificial intelligence is the operation of the telephone system as it encodes the voices and transmits the signals and decodes them into a form recognizable as human speech at the receiver.

As these examples indicate, the hallmarks of new superorganic agency are multiple participants that recombine in varying configurations for temporary periods. These attributes show up repeatedly in the characterizations produced by a variety of theorists in a variety of contexts. Haraway (1991) and Dumit and Davis-Floyd (1998:1) describe cyborgs as hybrid, indeterminate, and ambiguous in contrast to the stable, clearly defined, and bounded individuals who populate traditional worldview and drive methodological individualism. Robert Jay Lifton claims that today's self has become "protean," a dynamic, unstable being marked by fragmentation, fluidity, contingency, multiplicity, and polyvocality (Lifton 1993:8, 14–24). As we have seen in a previous chapter, the protean self is subject to its peculiar pathologies. Overall, however, Lifton assesses it in a positive light, honoring its "plurality and multiplicity" and "delighting in the partial and inconsistent meanings revealed by disparate forms and alternative ways of life" (Shweder 1994:16). Proteanism increases flexibility and, therefore, empathy for other people (Lifton 1993:214–15).

David Gunkel holds that communication, which involves multiple individuals and is often mediated by electronic or other technological devices, has always been the province of recombinant cyborgs (Gunkel 2000:340). "Borg subjectivities . . . are not conceptualized as preexisting, selfsame, or self-determining individuals. Rather, they are relational subjects constructed and reconstructed based on the vicissitudes of the network. . . . Borg subjects float, suspended between points of objectivity, being constituted and reconstituted in different configurations in relation to the discursive arrangement of the occasion" (p. 345). Similarly, Mark Poster perceives in the shift from written to electronically mediated communication a change in the subject from "an agent centered in rational/imaginary autonomy" to one that is "decentered, dispersed, and multiplied in continuous instability" (Poster 1990:6). A specific case is the notion of the unique author, which is fading as technological developments such as word processing and hypertext make it easy to modify written texts. These blur distinctions between the original author and readers, who are coming to be seen as jointly exercising the role of the author (Poster 1990:114–15, 2001:91–94; Landow 1997:90; Burbules and Callister 2000:44). One example is how the learner, software programmer, and computer all participate in the operation of interactive instructional programs, which pose different questions or tasks based on the learner's performance on previous ones (Bolter 1991:6).

The dynamic, recombinant quality of this concept of agency is consistent with the view of the world recommended by relativity and quantum theory. From that perspective, according to physicist David Bohm, everything is an unbroken flow of movement in which supposedly concrete and durable things such as observer and observed are only relatively invariant forms of movement that come together for a time to form wholes and then flow apart from each other into other wholes (Bohm 1980:xi, 47). "Complexity science," as represented by chaos theory, fractal geometry, and molecular biology, entails a similar view (Downey and Rogers 1995:271; Dillon 2000:9). Michael Dillon describes it in terms of "radical relationality"—the notion that everything exists as temporary, recombinant relationships. This view does not allow for unequivocal definitions and distinctions, as between machine and organism, or the human and nonhuman. What might be called slippages, deformations, or contamination from another perspective are not anomalous on this view but ordinary examples of how things work (Dillon 2000:4, 12–13).

Unlike the static, one-size-fits-all quality of methodological individualism's program to explain everything in terms of human individuals, the new superorganic gives all of the components involved in action their just due. It is designed to deal with the many combinations and permutations of human and artificial intelligence and human and artificial memory that have become commonplace in contemporary life. They are in play whenever one withdraws cash from an ATM, makes a telephone call, writes with a word processor, communicates by e-mail, visits Web sites, purchases something on the Internet or at the supermarket, and so on through a myriad of everyday activities. A full understanding of what is going on requires a superorganic model that recognizes how artificial intelligence now routinely supplements human intelligence.

It must be stressed that this in no way threatens to banish human beings from the scene, nor to diminish the individual. The participation of automation transforms agency from a human soliloquy to a conversation among several human and nonhuman participants. Apart from those activities that are managed exclusively by computers, the role of the individual remains indispensable; in fact, it is often expanded. The inclusion of artificial intelligence significantly increases the amount of information to take into consideration. As we have already seen, this places greater demands on human intelligence to evaluate the relevance of that information and encourages greater flexibility and creativity in its interpretation. This is an important element in automation's attack on closed culture, because flexibility and creativity include sensitivity to the possible merits of diverse ideas and practices. That opens culture and is conducive to the recognition of cultural differences as complementary rather than contradictory or compartmental, thus ameliorating the trouble with culture.

The concept of agency advanced here differs from methodological individualism in two fundamental ways. First, it is variable and contingent, differently composed in different circumstances. Second, it is superorganic, because its decision-making (information processing) activity often includes elements of artificial intelligence that are not reducible to human intelligence. It is, however, a *new* superorganic, because it does not recapitulate earlier notions of the superorganic either as groups considered entities apart from their members, or as reification of cultural beliefs and values into things that exist independently of the people who hold them. It refers instead to the empirical agencies that undertake social action. Although variable in composition, temporary in duration, and better understood as conjunctions for action than as fixed objects, these agencies are no less concrete than human beings themselves. They are made, in addition to flesh and blood, of plastic and metal, of silicon and lines of code.

Chapter 10

Opening Culture, Expanding Individuals

The various topics discussed in this book have circled around two issues: the proposition that culture has become a divisive force in contemporary society, and an investigation of the relevance of the automation of information to that situation. The proposition, which I have labeled the trouble with culture, is also the subject of a slim volume titled *Thick and Thin: Moral Argument at Home and Abroad*, published in 1994 by philosopher Michael Walzer. Essentially Walzer's argument is that when basic values—freedom, truth, fairness—are considered in the simplest, most general terms, people everywhere are in essential agreement about them. So, he states, anyone would identify with the cause of marchers in Prague in 1989, some of whom carried signs that simply said "Truth" or "Justice." However, elaborations on precisely what terms such as these mean bring any number of parochial cultural and historical considerations into play. These generate divergent interpretations that erode the consensus and may even produce sharp disagreement.

Walzer designates the values, in their general guise that evokes universal consensus, as "thin." Their locally elaborated, more variable, and more contentious versions are "thick." Walzer does not claim that thin values are the bases upon which thick ones are built. To the contrary, he insists that the thick, context-laden values come first, and that the thin ones are stripped-down abbreviations of them (Walzer 1994:10, 15). Thin values, that is, attract widespread assent, because they dwell in the areas of

153

overlap among thick ones and do not evoke entangling alliances with other concepts in elaborately structured systems. It is not exactly that they stand alone, but rather that they are expressed simply and generally enough that diverse people can agree about them without getting bogged down in their thicker, culturally variable contexts. The less an idea is expressed in rich terms involving other ideas, the more likely it is to garner general consensus.

Walzer's book, which boils down to a design for how people might get along more successfully in today's world, essentially calls for more emphasis on the thin values on which everyone agrees. This, he maintains, would produce more toleration for the differences among their thick elaborations, because when thick values (ours and others') are addressed from the perspective of their overlapping, thin versions, the differences among them are easier to understand and to swallow.

This book also is concerned with how people with cultural differences might coexist more harmoniously in the contemporary world, and some of the concepts we have developed have a good deal in common with Walzer's. Our distinction between closed and open culture, for example, shares something with his between thick and thin, for I have argued that when culture opens, it (like thinness) makes room for greater tolerance of different ways of thinking and behaving. The distinction between classifying and indexing, so critical to the present work, also is relevant here. Walzer holds that thick values are more thoroughly embedded in contexts than thin ones. We have analyzed classifying as a means of ordering information in more or less elaborate contexts and indexing in terms of matching particulars in the absence of context. Thus as far as context is concerned, thick concepts and values are like classifying, and thin ones are like indexing.

Rich contexts are the fruit of more or less extended historical developments within particular geographic regions (Western Europe, Tahiti), religious or philosophical traditions (Christianity, Islam, utilitarianism), social classes (proletariat, peasantry, aristocracy), occupational categories (the military, the intelligentsia), and the like. They are the stuff of which culture is made, and it is the nature of rich contexts to direct the course of thinking along preestablished, culturally sanctioned channels. These channels, consisting of constellations of associated concepts that may be described in terms of Walzer's thick values or our classification schemes, are often deep enough that it is difficult to see outside them. In such cases, while culture may create a high degree of internal accord, it does so by regulating thought to the point of shutting out alternatives. These are viewed with intolerance or hostility, producing all of the ills that we have associated with contradictory and compartmental differences. And that, of course, is the trouble with culture.

Thin values and the products of indexing, on the other hand, have minimal contexts. The former do have them, but they are deemphasized; the latter stand alone, without contexts, because they originate from the matching of particulars. This minimizing or absence of context loosens the grip of culture on thought. Because they bring minimal baggage, lightly contexted ideas can be criticized and entertained without prejudice, and their implications can be explored, all with a reduced likelihood of contradicting allied notions. Thus Walzer and this book are saying essentially the same thing: when context is minimized (by thinning down to the overlapping essentials, or by accessing information by indexing rather than classification), the possibilities of creative thinking, mutual understanding, and tolerance increase, and the trouble with culture is alleviated.

Still, this book differs from what Walzer did, in three ways. First, it extends the analysis to cover a broader spectrum of human experience. Thick or thin, the values that concern Walzer ring of existential importance: truth, justice, freedom, and the like. On the other hand, our casting of the analysis in terms of classifying and indexing makes it applicable to the full gamut of facts, values, and concepts that engage human beings, ranging from the momentous to the mundane. Second, it demonstrates that the most likely candidate to bring about the shift toward greater thinness or openness is not directly through a change in ways of thinking but indirectly, by a change in habitual behavior brought about by innovations in information technology. Third, it places these matters in the evolutionary history of human society and culture.

The second difference is the reason for the first: it is precisely because the source of change is to be found in new behavioral habits that its effects are as much or more visible in mundane matters as in existentially weighty ones. Here, indeed, lies a problem with Walzer's analysis. I do not think a lasting and meaningful edifice of mutual respect and understanding can be built from the starting point of thinned-down foundational principles of thinking and valuing such as Truth, Justice, and Freedom. They thicken the moment people start to think about or discuss them with any degree of seriousness, and that invites the very disagreements that Walzer wants to avoid.

It seems to me that there are only two ways to keep issues such as these at the center of the process, neither of which is very promising. One is to ask people to understand and respect the differences between the many varieties of Truth, Justice, and the rest in their full thickness. This is the strategy of cultural relativism, which stresses that alien beliefs and values can be understood and appreciated only in the richness of their cultural contexts. The other is to convince people that there really are not any thick values at all, that all of them are ultimately and irrevocably thin. This is one way of expressing the strategy of postmodernism, with its emphasis on indeterminacy and relationships among signifiers that never come to rest at any solid thing or principle. The discussion in chapter 3 reached the conclusion that not many people are willing to adopt either of these courses—relativism, because it asks too much of people, both in terms of the time and effort required to reach a full understanding of alien beliefs and practices, and because some of those beliefs and practices are so repellant to outsiders on their face that they have no wish to do anything but condemn them outright, and postmodernism, because it leaves people with too little in the way of deep principles on which they can ground their convictions about pivotal matters such as Truth and Justice and the meaning of life. I doubt that Walzer would see either of these strategies as a viable solution to the problem either. He would not opt for the relativist approach, because he thinks that, far from leading to better understanding, it is precisely the thickness of values and concepts that lies at the heart of disagreements and conflict. Nor would he accept the postmodernist solution, because he holds that thick values definitely exist and, in fact, that they came first, and that thin ones are just abridged versions of them.

My contention is that the road to greater tolerance and mutual understanding begins not with the weightiest of values but technologically induced changes in habitual thought and behavior. Thus we have looked first at new technologies of information management, and next to their immediate, if not existentially dramatic, consequences for how information is organized, acquired, and interpreted. Habitual changes in these matters lead to more general shifts in how people think and view the world, including but by no means limited to, the momentous issues of Truth, Justice, and Freedom. A softening of the contradictory and compartmental differences that underpin the trouble with culture is one of the indirect consequences—or by-products—of these technologically induced changes. Thus this book takes its place among those studies holding that enduring and far-reaching changes in ways of thinking and believing are more likely to be engendered indirectly by developments in the material conditions of life than directly from seeds sown in ideology itself.

This book's third extension of Walzer's discussion—placing the issues in the context of the evolution of society and culture—itself requires more extended treatment. The gist of the argument has been that in the early phases of human existence, culture was well adapted to small-scale, homogeneous societies with a minimal division of labor. The common understandings, values, and customs of culture provided the commonality of thought and behavior, the mechanical solidarity that held such societies together and distinguished them from each other. This state of affairs is most fully realized when culture is closed, establishing the mind-set that cultural premises about what is true and what is false and what is good and what is evil must be embraced unquestioningly.

All that worked well enough when societies were small, with little internal cultural diversity, and did not encounter each other very often. But the evolutionary paths of society and culture have gone in separate directions. Society has changed a great deal, evolving from small, relatively isolated, face-to-face groups with cultural homogeneity to huge nation states linked in a global system, with complex divisions of labor and a great deal of internal cultural diversity expressed as differences in ethnicity, class, education, occupation, religion, and ideology. Until recently, culture, for its part, has changed relatively little. It has remained a set of common understandings, values, and customs that flourishes when its adherents fully accept its principles and support them dogmatically. As a result of their evolutionary divergence, the relationship between society and culture has become strained. When the mind-set associated with closed culture and dependent individuals is carried forward into large-scale societies, culture becomes a disruptive force. Just a few examples are *idées fixes* about God's establishment of marriage as a relationship exclusively between one man and one woman, the war on terror as a prelude to Armageddon, and the heavenly reward for becoming a suicide bomber in Israel or Iraq. While the results are often not as extreme as some of these examples, it is the nature of closed culture to breed individuals who are dependent. They have difficulty thinking outside of their received cultural categories. They feel threatened by other points of view, against which they mount either a vigorous defense or steadfast refusal even to consider them. This defensiveness and exclusiveness encourage perception of the cultural differences within and between societies as contradictory or compartmental. Culturally different groups confront each other with hostility, or they dismiss each other with indifference. That is the trouble with culture.

The antidote is for individuals to become more independent and for culture to become more open. When this happens, it does not mean that culture teeters on the edge of extinction, or even that it narrows in scope. Culture maintains its body of premises and understandings. Durkheim says that these become more general and indeterminate (1933:172). This may be true in some cases, but I think the more salient factor is that, whether its precepts are general or specific, open culture relinquishes much of its authority—not that people reject or disregard their culture, but that they are no longer in thrall to it to the point that they are threatened by the existence of different ways of thinking; they are able to contemplate them dispassionately. When foreign ways flatly contradict their own culture, people usually reject the other and continue to affirm their own, although sometimes they might reach the opposite conclusion. When, as is much more common, the divergent ideas and practices are not incompatible, open-minded people consider them all and frequently discern common ground or mutually beneficial accommodations among them. In that circumstance, cultural differences often appear complementary, and this leads to greater understanding and a more cooperative, constructive state of affairs in complex societies.

The foregoing chapters have argued that one factor conducive to opening culture is the automation of information. It does not do so, as the largely unsuccessful relativism and postmodernism do, by mounting a frontal, ideological assault on closed culture. Instead, it is a technological innovation that has transformed the management of information. Prior to automation, information was managed in the oral and textual modes, where human intelligence processes information stored in human and artificial memory, the latter consisting of written texts, graphic images, and the like. In the automated mode of information management, information stored in artificial memory (such as digitalized databases) is processed by artificial intelligence. The participation of the automated mode in information management is bringing about important changes that work to open culture. These changes are found mainly in two cultural regions: agency and ways of thinking.

By "agency" I mean simply how things get done. As discussed in chapter 9, the automated mode of information management forces us to change the way we think about that. Previously the things that act were considered distinct and durable, separable from what they do. Thus under the popular approach of methodological individualism, the fundamental agent was considered to be the human individual, and any given individual was the same agent as it did many different things: ate, prayed, joined groups, conversed with other individuals, worked, weighed and considered ideas, and so on. The limitations of this view, which have always existed, have been brought sharply into focus by automation. Perhaps this is because our lack of autonomy of action becomes starkly obvious from our helplessness to do anything when the computers go down. In any event, it is now becoming apparent that a more fluid concept of agency is needed. As I use it, "agency" refers to something doing something; that is, some entity or combination of entities engaging in some activity.

This is different from the earlier view, on two counts. First, it does not draw a bright line between what is done and who or what does it. It includes both the activity and the performing entities in the concept of agency, because neither can stand alone. A football team has no existence apart from the games, practices, meetings, banquets, and other activities it engages in, and a football game has no existence apart from the teams that play it (among other things, such as a suitable field and the presence of a football).

The second difference, following from the first, is that the part of agency consisting of entities that perform actions cannot be considered unitary and durable, such as a human individual. They consist of composite, superorganic entities combining human, mechanical, and other elements rather than the individual of methodological individualism acting alone. Moreover, their composition changes according to the activity. The agency that undertakes my present activity of composing this text, consisting of myself, a computer, and a word processing program, is different from the agency that will be in play in an hour or so when my wife and I sit down together to have lunch and discuss the events of the morning.

Thus methodological individualism's stable, determinate individual loses its pride of place. In its stead arise indeterminate, ad hoc agencies consisting of any combination of human and nonhuman components formed to accomplish a particular activity, dissolve when it is finished, and form again in different configurations to undertake other activities. Prime examples, as discussed in chapter 8, are the case-specific teams and practice groups in law firms, multidisciplinary groups formed to undertake particular scientific research projects, interdisciplinary programs in

universities, virtual project teams in business, and just-in-time, agile manufacturing techniques.

As with its effect on agency, automation also has fostered changes in
information management. And the changes have moved in the same direction: from determinacy and stability toward indeterminacy and fluidity. In
information management, the changes turn on the shift from the prominence of classification in the oral and textual modes to the importance of
indexing in the automated mode. Earlier chapters have explored the many
ramifications of this shift. Especially important is that information
derived from classified sources is always already sorted according to the
categories of a preestablished, stable classificatory scheme. Thus the significance of the information the user receives has been determined in
advance by those who classified it as they did. On the other hand, and in
common with superorganic agencies in accordance with the specific activities they undertake, with indexing, the information that is acquired and
applied is uniquely selected with reference to each circumstance. Compared to the use of classified materials, the process is indeterminate and
fluid. Just what information one receives depends on the formulation of
specific search queries, which vary between different users and even
between the same users at different times. Conclusions are less foregone,
because it is up to the user to identify connections between bits of information and to discern whatever pattern or general significance may reside
in them. The obligation of users to reach their own interpretations may
result in novel insights and construals.

Thus it becomes clear that the automation of information has parallel consequences for both ways of thinking and agency. In both, fixed,
one-size-fits-all categories are broken down in favor of fluid, ad hoc ways
of thinking and acting tailored to particular problems and activities.
When thinking incorporates the automated mode, it encourages, even
demands, flexibility and creativity of interpretation by human intelligence
to cope with the query-specific and novel juxtapositions of information
that are often produced by the indexing techniques of automated searching. Just-in-time practices and organizational strategies such as interdisciplinary scientific research projects and virtual project teams in business
and law are task-specific juxtapositions of knowledge and skills featuring
that same flexibility. If they are to work effectively, they too demand more
creativity and initiative from the human beings participating in them.
Clearly fixed categories and permanent agents suit the more rigid condi-

tions of closed culture, while fluidity and indeterminacy in both thinking and agency are conducive to open culture. Therefore, an important consequence of automation is to nudge people away from the constraints of closed culture, to make them more open-minded, and thus to alleviate the trouble with culture by increasing the probability that they will perceive cultural differences as complementary rather than contradictory or compartmental.

This book has considered in any depth developments in only a few areas of contemporary society: the law, scholarship, and, to a considerably lesser extent, business and manufacturing practices. Automation has obviously touched much more than that, and if there is merit in my general hypothesis that automation encourages greater openness and flexibility in agency and in thinking, then similar tendencies should be visible in architecture, engineering, medicine, journalism, the military, and in many other places. Moreover, although my intention has been to analyze the roots of what is happening now rather than to make predictions about the future, what we have been talking about is a relatively recent innovation that shows every sign of continuing to expand its influence indefinitely. Therefore, I allow myself the modest prediction that, again if the hypothesis is sound, as time passes the kind of developments we have been discussing will become more pervasive and influential.

Moving from particular predictions to the much more general issue of the overall trajectory of cultural evolution, our conclusions leave us in a peculiar position. The innovation of automated information technology is a step in cultural evolution, but what I have drawn from it points in the opposite direction from many other recent analyses of that subject. From the Renaissance and the Enlightenment into the twentieth century, the predominant view was the humanist one, that history is the story of the progressive liberation and self-actualization of the human individual. But many more recent scholars have been persuaded by the contrary view, that change originates in the material conditions of life, and that human beings are relatively helpless chips borne along by the currents of cultural evolution. Leslie White, for example, held that culture follows its own evolutionary trajectory, independent of the intentions of human beings, and not necessarily for their benefit. Writing in the aftermath of World War II, but with cause that (despite current ostrich-like complacency) is at least as urgent today, he questioned the survival of human civilization if the power of nuclear energy should again be used in war (White 1949:338–40, 350,

358; Barrett 1989). An anti-humanist theme removing the human subject from a central position in history gathered momentum in the latter-twentieth-century theories of structuralism and poststructuralism (Best and Kellner 1991:19–20, 24). Thus in a debate over the driving force in the Marxian view of the historical dialectic, John Lewis championed the earlier humanist tradition by identifying it as human striving to overcome bondage and alienation and to achieve freedom, justice, and equality. Louis Althusser, taking a poststructuralist perspective, insisted that the engine of history is the class struggle, perceived as a force in itself quite independent of any human intentions or aspirations (Althusser 1976:46–54). Finally, the influential social theorist Michel Foucault (1977) argued in *Discipline and Punish* that the evolution of "technologies of power" over the last three or four centuries should be understood not in terms of any human purpose but as the self-actualization of Power, understood as a thing in itself that increasingly perfects its techniques of surveillance and domination. Indeed, for Foucault, the human subject, understood as a social being with certain attributes such as free will, individual identity, dignity, intelligence, and political rights and duties, is itself the product of a certain historical era rather than a being who transcends and/or guides history (Foucault 1984:59, 1970:387).

The interesting thing is that the present analysis of the automation of information suggests that materialist means serve humanist ends. Although human beings are no less involuntarily carried along by this particular sequence of changes than by those following any other technological innovation, this time the upshot is to strengthen and liberate rather than to marginalize the individual. This is most definitely not to say that the individual is an independent agent and the sole author of social action. I have argued strenuously against that methodological individualist view and held to the contrary that individuals are participants in larger agencies that also comprise, depending on the circumstances, other individuals, plants, animals, machines, databases, landforms, the weather, and so on. I also have acknowledged that narrowcast mass media, the Internet, and other automated resources can be and often are used to make many people even more dependent on the premises of their closed cultures. But the major thrust of my argument has been on the other side. When used for professional and investigative purposes, automated techniques call upon the interpretive powers of human intelligence to play an enlarged role, one that liberates the individual from uncritical adherence to the categories of culture. This is a useful reminder that there is nothing in the notion of cultural evolution starting from material causes and proceeding independently of human beings that requires the increasing subjugation of the individual, or even the gathering dominance of culture itself. In principle, change may take the opposite course, and this time it does.

The consequences of automation also indicate that, after millennia of divergence, the evolution of culture and the evolution of society may be moving toward realignment. Culture's emphasis on clarity, permanence, and unquestioning allegiance, which had served small, relatively isolated societies well, became disruptive and divisive as society evolved toward greater size, complexity, and diversity. The introduction of the textual mode of information management, a step in cultural evolution fueled by the technological developments of writing and printing, had little effect on culture's penchant to be closed and, therefore, did little to ameliorate the increasing incompatibilities between culture and society. But the automated mode of information management fosters the rise of indexing and the decline of classifying as the predominant means of organizing and accessing information, and that tends to open culture by encouraging the recognition of cultural differences as complementary rather than contradictory or compartmental. Simultaneously, the automated mode mitigates the tendency of methodological individualism to see individuals as isolated from and often set against each other. To the contrary, its consonance with superorganic agency emphasizes the complementary interdependence of individuals with each other and with other living or inanimate beings. All of this diminishes divisiveness within and between large, complex, internally diverse societies and thus constitutes an evolutionary move toward the reconciliation of culture with society.

Notes

CHAPTER 1

1. An exception is anthropologist Jules Henry's (1963) critique of American culture, *Culture against Man*. Some parts of the remainder of this chapter have appeared in Hanson (2005). I am grateful to Transaction Publishers for permission to include them here.

CHAPTER 2

1. For a more complete discussion of the history of poverty and the meanings associated with it, see Hanson (1997).

2. In a footnote, however, Smith qualifies this by noting that some newsgroups are created globally but distribute messages regionally, so the server he used may not have picked up some contributions.

CHAPTER 3

1. A few semi-anthropologists and philosophers of anthropology who retain a hankering toward unilineal evolutionism, such as Ernest Gellner (1992) and Ian Jarvie (1964, 1984), are exceptions to this.

2. But see Shweder (2002).

3. For the record, I should point out that I am personally not persuaded by these criticisms of relativism. I think that a coherent and an acceptable desirable account of relativism can be fashioned, and I have made various efforts in that direction (Hanson 1975, 1979, 1981, 1985, 1995; Hanson and Martin 1973). But none of that mitigates the point I am trying to make here: there are good reasons that, despite efforts (including my own) to make it palatable and convincing, cultural relativism does not enjoy wide acceptance.

Therefore, as a practical matter, it is not a promising candidate to alleviate the trouble with culture.

4. Again, my own view of postmodernism is much more positive than the criticisms reviewed here; indeed, I think it can make a positive contribution to empirical social science (see Hanson 1989, 1997). But, as with relativism, my concern here is to point out postmodernism's general unpopularity.

5. From ancient times through the Renaissance, "artificial memory" referred to "the art of memory," that is, the cultivated or trained memory, as contrasted with "natural memory" that everyone has from birth (Yates 1966:5). In the terminology I am using, that sense of "artificial memory" is part of human memory.

6. Of course, it is not necessary to talk out loud for human intelligence to process information stored in human memory. It is often done silently. I use "oral" in the sense of "oral tradition," a well-known concept that refers to knowledge that is not set down in writing.

CHAPTER 4

1. Located some 700 miles southeast of Tahiti, Rapa is a high, volcanic island, covering an area of about ten square miles. When my wife and I did fieldwork there in 1964, Rapa's population was 360.

2. The following description of the significance of location on Rapa is based on Hanson 1970:46–47.

3. Elsewhere in Polynesia, the use of space as an organizing principle has been described for the Cook Islands (Crocombe 1964:20–21), New Zealand (Hanson and Hanson 1983:65), Rangiroa (Ottino 1972:276–78), and French Polynesia generally (Panoff 1964:118–20).

4. An interesting Web site is http://www.friesian.com/elements.htm (accessed April 18, 2002) which describes several additional correspondence classification systems from Greece, India, and China.

5. The debate over the generality of taxonomic classification and its relation to human cognition and culture has generated a large literature in anthropology. A few high points are Ellen and Reason (1979), Berlin, Breedlove and Raven (1973), Berlin (1992), Needham (1979), Sahlins (1976), Lopez et al. (1997), and Kay (1971).

6. In fact, pre-European Tahitians did have the bow and arrow, although it was used primarily for contests to see who could shoot the farthest, only occasionally for hunting and not for warfare (Oliver 1974:1:320).

7. For discussions of some of them, see Lovejoy (1964), Dolby (1979), Machlup (1982), Slaughter (1982), and Kelley and Popkin (1991).

8. Augustine imagined that the three powers of the human mind—memory, understanding, and will—reflected the structure of the divine Trinity (Yates 1966:49).

9. Huarte entertained many interesting notions, including the one that bright children tend to be born of dull fathers. Wise men, he explained, often have slow children, because they do not devote themselves vigorously to the task of copulating, their minds being preoccupied with loftier subjects. Dull men, on the other hand, "apply themselves affectionately to the carnal act, and are not carried away to any other contemplation." Thus they produce strong seed that results in bright progeny (Huarte 1959:286).

10. Woodward's (1816) scheme is summarized in his Table 1. Its various categories are discussed throughout the work, especially pp. 248–98, 309, and 345–62. An interesting element in his scheme is the dialectical tactic of distinguishing between a pair of opposites (thesis and antithesis) and then defining a third term (synthesis) as a combination of them. This appears at least twice: in the three provinces themselves and again in the three orders of Ennoeica.

11. "The Library of Babel," a short story by Jorge Luis Borges, is a delightful rumination on this subject.

12. See the Web site http://www.fisher.lib.virginia.edu/cgi-local/arlbin/arl.cgi?task=setupreport (accessed February 21, 2002).

13. It could be argued that classifications by correspondence do not really deal in particulars, because the concepts "red wolf" or "liver" are already abstractions or generalizations derived from a group of concrete animals or internal organs. This is true, but I hold that the proclivity to abstract is more pronounced in taxonomic systems, where concepts such as these are generalized still further at higher levels in the hierarchy.

CHAPTER 5

1. Some sections of this chapter and chapter 8 appeared in Hanson (2002), which offers a more detailed treatment of legal research and the impact of automation on it.

2. Grossman (1994) reproduces a series of previously published "selections" on the history of legal research from a variety of sources, with connective tissue in the form of "notes" by Grossman himself. When citations are to selections, I will include a footnote identifying the original source. Citations to Grossman's own notes will not be accompanied by footnotes. This particular citation is to a selection by J. H. Baker, "Records, Reports, and the Origins of Case-Law in England," in J. H. Baker, ed., *Law Records and the Growth of Case Law* (Berlin: Dunker and Humblot, 1989), 15–21.

3. The original source is the Report of the Committee on Law Reporting of the Association of the Bar of the City of New York, 1873.

4. This citation from Grossman, and the next one, are from J. Abramson, J. Kennedy, and E. J. Pollock, "Inside the West Empire," *The American Lawyer* (October 1983):5:90–95.

5. Treatises are book-length surveys and analyses of particular areas of the law, such as *Corbin on Contracts*, *Wigmore on Evidence*, and *Prosser on Torts*. *Restatements* was a project launched by the American Law Institute in the 1920s to standardize the application of

the law by clearly setting out fundamental principles, illustrating how they should be applied, and precisely defining the proper meaning of basic legal terms. There are now restatements for seventeen areas of law, most of which consist of several thick volumes.

6. The foregoing information regarding the workings of the West National Reporter and American Digest systems is taken primarily from Doyle (1992:231–32), Grossman (1994:76–81, 83), Cohen (1985:34–47, 60–70), and my own use of the systems.

7. Berring's effusiveness regarding the impact of the West classification system on the structure of American law is not shared by everyone. For a thoughtful rejoinder, see Schanck (1990a:17–19).

8. The seven "grand categories" in the West system are persons, property, contracts, torts, crimes, remedies, and government (Bintliff 1996:342). A check of the first-year curriculum of sixteen law schools from different regions and ranked tiers reveals that all of them require courses on civil procedure, contracts, and torts, fifteen require courses on property and criminal law, and nine require a course on constitutional law. All sixteen also require a course on legal analysis. The only other courses in the first-year curriculum are "Pretrial Advocacy" and "Law, Culture, and Difference," each offered by only one school.

9. This point was made by Kent McKeever, director of the Columbia University Law Library, during an interview.

CHAPTER 6

1. As it happens, the full text of *Following the Equator* is now available at http://www.gutenberg.net/etext/2895. I did search it for "round man" on September 15, 2004, and I found the quote quickly. Some parts of this chapter have previously appeared in Hanson (2004a). I acknowledge the Taylor & Francis Group for permission to include them here.

2. There are, of course, classifications of things and people as well as of material in documents. But when it is recalled that what is being classified is not exactly things or people in themselves but ideas about them, it is fair to speak generally of organizing bits of information.

3. Keith Shafer, "A Brief Introduction to Scorpion," http://www.orc.rsch.oclc.org: 6109/bintro.html (accessed June 2, 2002).

4. Northern Light began to narrow its services in the spring of 2002, when it ceased searching the Internet and limited itself to documents in its own "general collection," which it delivered to users on a pay-as-you-go basis. (For the most part, the cost was modest—from $1 to $4 per document. The highest fee I have seen is $1,600.) The search engine virtually disappeared when its owning company went bankrupt in 2003, but later that year it began restructuring under new ownership for use by business customers (Hollmer 2003).

5. Another product that also automatically classifies documents according to a predefined taxonomic scheme is "Quiver" (Wiggins 2002:61–63, 65). It is more customized

than Northern Light, designed to categorize corporate intranet documents according to schemes devised by each customer. Although it is on the market, it can hardly be said to be in widespread use, because its price starts at $125,000.

6. See Dreyfus (1992:xvi-xxx) for an argument that the Cyc Project is misguided in principle.

7. I am using the same example as my source, "Hits and Misses" (1998). It states that the search for "jaguar" also will turn up documents about a football team. But no sites pertaining to the Jacksonville Jaguars were included in the first ten pages of my search on Google on February 26, 2004. They do appear in abundance in a search for "jaguars."

8. A single document might end up in more than one cluster if it is similar to other documents in one cluster in one way and to documents in another cluster in another way.

9. See http://www.vivisimo.com/faq/Technology.html (accessed June 25, 2004).

10. Another application of potential relevance here is DolphinSearch. This product uses neural net technology to ascertain the meaning of words and documents through pattern recognition, which enables it to weed out irrelevant documents in a Web search and also to automatically classify documents (Wiggins 2002:63–65; Roitblat 2000). Its parallel to clustering and HITS, Roitblat stresses, is that DolphinSearch classifies not according to some preestablished taxonomic scheme but to the particular needs of the user at the moment (Roitblat 2000:3–4, 9). As with Quiver, DolphinSearch is hardly in general use, being limited to those large law firms and corporations that can afford its six-figure cost.

CHAPTER 7

1. Although classifications by correspondence do not take a tree form, they also connect items along preestablished paths.

2. Another way of expressing this is with the concept "informate," a term attributed to Professor Shoshana Zuboff of the Harvard Business School. Automation encourages the development of new insights by "informating" data, that is, establishing an environment in which data may be applied in a variety of ways other than the original intention (DiMarco 1997).

3. This phrasing occurs repeatedly in the results of a Google search for "definition of hypertext."

4. This was curious, because generally Google returns vastly more results than a metasearch engine such as Vivisimo. Presumably the reason was that Vivisimo consults several search engines, and with a query as narrow as this one, it could accept all of the findings of each and still remain within the fairly small number of findings it generally reports.

5. The "*" is a wildcard marker to include both "rafter" and "rafters." This function is not available on many of the other databases, so I had to conduct separate searches with "rafter" and "rafters," although with no better results.

6. I tried the same thing for two other search engines. Interestingly, Altavista was similar to Google in this regard, but the results on Lycos began to lose their relevance to the query after about 400.

7. I say "most of" because the final cluster in the primary Vivisimo list is called "other topics," a potpourri of sites not included in any of the other clusters. In contrast, the clustering metasearch engines, Excite, Dogpile, MetaCrawler, and WebCrawler, present all of their findings in named clusters.

8. I stress the "as if" element of this, because when I tried actually refining a Vivisimo query to include the cluster name as an AND search term, the results were not at all limited to the items in the cluster. Unfortunately I did not think to try this with my first examples until some time after I had done the original trials, and (true to the varying clusters that one gets for the same search at different times with metasearch engines) when I searched Vivisimo for Tuamotu OR Tuamotuan months later, there was no cluster "Pitcairn Island." Nor did a search for Clifford Geertz return a cluster "ethnocentrism." Trying it with another example, a Vivisimo search for "cultural relativism" on June 26, 2004, produced a cluster of four items labeled "valid." I then entered the new search query "'cultural relativism' AND valid" and received well over 100 results. The four that appeared in the "valid" cluster in my original search were included in the list of results of the second search as numbers 6, 12, 17, and 19.

9. See http://www.vivisimo.com/products/Enterprise_Publisher/Introduction. html (accessed March 12, 2004).

CHAPTER 8

1. But see Berman (1993:290) for a very different notion of legal positivism.

2. See, however, Lien (1998:90) for a claim that automated research is congenial to "extreme positivists."

3. Schanck (1990a) has criticized Barkan's article for going too far, but on this point the distance between them does not appear too great (see pp. 10–11; see also Barkan 1990; Schanck 1990b).

4. The schools in our survey include Brooklyn, California Berkeley, Chicago Kent, Dickinson, Iowa, Maryland, Mercer, Miami, Oregon, South Dakota, Texas, Toledo, Tulane, University of Washington, Washington University St. Louis, and Yale.

5. The University of Iowa and Yale are not included in this comparison because although both encourage joint degrees, their published information does not give specifics about particular interdisciplinary programs.

6. The journals we examined were the *American Anthropologist, American Journal of Sociology, American Journal of Psychology, American Historical Review, American Economic Review, American Political Science Review, MLN, Language, Journal of Philosophy,* and *American Journal of Philology.*

7. See http://www.nsf.gov/home/crssprgm/hsd/start.htm (accessed March 23, 2004).

8. Now known as the Program in European Cultural Studies.

9. As with any innovation, not all of its representatives "take." An inspection of the Alaska Pacific Web site in September 2003 revealed that this curriculum is no longer current.

10. See http://www.kawasaki.com/about/kmm_lincoln.html (accessed April 29, 2004).

11. DiMaggio gives the publication date 1996 for Sabel's and Zeitlin's book, but all references to the work that I could find indicate that it was published in 1997.

12. See http://dora.eeap.cwru.edu/agile/home.html, the Agile Manufacturing Project of the Center for Automation and Intelligent Systems Research, Case Western Reserve University (accessed March 22, 2005).

CHAPTER 9

1. Parts of this chapter have appeared in an article of the same name in *Current Anthropology* (Hanson 2004b). I acknowledge the University of Chicago Press for permission to include them here.

2. Richard H. Jones's *Reductionism: Analysis and the Fullness of Reality* (2000) is an excellent study of the several varieties of methodological individualism.

3. For a different perspective on the rise and fall of the individual, see Kamenka's and Tay's contrast among three legal administrative traditions: *Gemeinschaft, Gesellschaft,* and bureaucratic-administrative (1975:129–42).

4. Terms such as self, individual, subject, and ego should in some circumstances be carefully distinguished. That is not the case here, because I am concerned only with their common reference to the individual human being understood as the basic unit of social action.

5. See www.microsoft.com/NTServer/appservice/techdetails/overview/msmqrev guide.asp (accessed February 10, 2001).

6. That children think of inanimate objects as alive, however, is anything but new. For generations they have imagined dolls and stuffed animals, railroad engines (not only today's Thomas and Percy but yesterday's "little engine that could"), and any number of other toys to be alive.

Bibliography

Althusser, Louis. 1976. *Essays in Self-Criticism.* London: NLB.

Appadurai, Arjun. 1996. *Modernity at Large: Cultural Dimensions of Globalization.* Minneapolis: University of Minnesota Press.

Arnold, Stephen E., and Michael Colson. 2000. The "R" Technology Revolution: Relationship, Research, Revenue. *Searcher* 8:36–52.

Bacon, Francis. 1605. *The Advancement of Learning.* London: Henrie Tomes.

Baker, Wayne. 2005. *America's Crisis of Values: Reality and Perception.* Princeton, NJ: Princeton University Press.

Baldi, Pierre. 2001. *The Shattered Self: The End of Natural Evolution.* Cambridge: MIT Press.

Barkan, Steven M. 1987. Deconstructing Legal Research: A Law Librarian's Commentary on Critical Legal Studies. *Law Library Journal* 79:617–37.

———. 1990. Response to Schanck: On the Need for Critical Law Librarianship, or Are We All Legal Realists Now? *Law Library Journal* 82:23–35.

Barrett, Richard A. 1989. The Paradoxical Anthropology of Leslie White. *American Anthropologist* 91:986–99.

Barton, Tamsyn. 1994. *Ancient Astrology.* London: Routledge.

Bast, Carol M., and Ransford C. Pyle. 2001. Legal Research in the Computer Age: A Paradigm Shift? *Law Library Journal* 93:285–302.

Bateson, Gregory. 1972a. Form, Substance, and Difference. In *Steps to an Ecology of Mind,* ed. G. Bateson, 448–66. New York: Ballantine.

———. 1972b. *Steps to an Ecology of Mind.* New York: Ballantine.

Baudrillard, Jean. 1998. The End of Millennium, or the Countdown. *Theory Culture and Society* 15:1–9.

Becher, Tony. 1989. *Academic Tribes and Territories: Intellectual Inquiry and the Culture of Disciplines.* Buckingham, UK: SRHE and Open University Press.

Becker, Barbara, and Josef Wehner. 2001. Electronic Networks and Civil Society: Reflections on Structural Changes in the Public Sphere. In *Culture, Technology,*

173

Communication: Towards an Intercultural Global Village, ed. Charles Ess and Fay Sudweeks, 67–85. Albany: State University of New York Press.

Belbin, Meredith. 1996. *The Coming Shape of Organization.* Oxford: Butterworth-Heinemann.

Belew, Richard K. 2000. *Finding Out About: A Cognitive Perspective on Search Engine Technology and the WWW.* Cambridge: Cambridge University Press.

Benedict, Ruth. 1934. *Patterns of Culture.* Boston: Houghton Mifflin.

Berlin, Brent. 1992. *Ethnobiological Classification: Principles of Categorization of Plants and Animals in Traditional Societies.* Princeton, NJ: Princeton University Press.

Berlin, Brent, Dennis Breedlove, and Peter H. Raven. 1973. General Principles of Classification and Nomenclature in Folk Biology. *American Anthropologist* 75:214–42.

Berman, Harold J. 1993. *Faith and Order: The Reconciliation of Law and Religion.* Atlanta: Scholars Press.

Berners-Lee, Tim, with Mark Fischetti. 1999. *Weaving the Web.* New York: HarperSanFrancisco.

Berners-Lee, Tim, James Hendler, and Ora Lassila. 2002 [2001]. The Semantic Web. In *The Future of the Web* 24–30. *Scientific American,* special online issue, no. 2. http://www.scientificamerican.com/special/toc.cfm?issueid=2&sc=rt_nav_list (accessed July 14, 2003).

Berring, Robert C. 1986. Full-Text Databases and Legal Research: Backing into the Future. *High Technology Law Journal* 1:27–60.

———. 1987. Legal Research and Legal Concepts: Where Form Molds Substance. *California Law Review* 75:15–27.

———. 1994. Collapse of the Structure of the Legal Research Universe: The Imperative of Digital Information. *Washington Law Review* 69:9–34.

Best, Steven, and Douglas Kellner. 1991. *Postmodern Theory: Critical Interrogations.* New York: Guildford Press.

Bintliff, Barbara. 1996. From Creativity to Computerese: Thinking Like a Lawyer in the Computer Age. *Law Library Journal* 88:338–51.

Bohm, David. 1980. *Wholeness and the Implicate Order.* London: Routledge & Kegan Paul.

Bolter, J. David. 1984. *Turing's Man: Western Culture in the Computer Age.* Chapel Hill: University of North Carolina Press.

———. 1991. *Writing Space: The Computer, Hypertext, and the History of Writing.* Hillsdale, NJ: Lawrence Erlbaum.

Bowker, Geoffrey C., and Susan Leigh Star. 1999. *Sorting Things Out: Classification and Its Consequences.* Cambridge: MIT Press.

Burbules, Nicholas C., and Thomas A. Callister, Jr. 2000. *Watch IT: The Risks and Promises of Information Technology for Education.* Boulder, CO: Westview Press.

Bibliography 175

Burckhardt, Jacob. 1954 [1860]. *The Civilization of the Renaissance in Italy.* New York: Modern Library.

Callon, Michel. 1987. Society in the Making: The Study of Technology As a Tool for Sociological Analysis. In *The Social Construction of Technological Systems: New Directions in the Sociology and History of Technology,* ed. W. E. Bijker, T. P. Hughes, and T. J. Pinch, 83–103. Cambridge: MIT Press.

———. 1999. Actor-Network Theory—The Market Test. In *Actor Network Theory and After,* ed. J. Law, and J. Hassard, 181–95. Oxford: Blackwell.

Cassiodorus, Senator. 1946. *An Introduction to Divine and Human Readings.* New York: Columbia University Press.

Castells, Manuel. 1997. *The Information Age: Economy, Society, and Culture, vol. 2, The Power of Identity.* 3 vols. Oxford: Blackwell.

———. 1998. *The Information Age: Economy, Society and Culture, vol. 3, End of the Millennium.* 3 vols. Oxford: Blackwell.

———. 2000 [1996]. *The Information Age: Economy, Society and Culture, vol. 1, The Rise of the Network Society.* 2d ed. 3 vols. Oxford: Blackwell.

Chakrabarti, S., B. Dom, D. Gibson, J. Kleinberg, P. Raghavan and S. Rajagopalan. 1998. *Automatic Resource Compilation by Analyzing Hyperlink Structure and Associated Text. Proceedings of the 7th World Wide Web Conference, 1998.:* Amsterdam: Elsevier Sciences.

Clanchy, M. T. 1993 [1979]. *From Memory to Written Records: England 1066–1307.* 2d ed. Oxford: Blackwell.

Clark, Andy. 2003. *Natural-Born Cyborgs: Minds, Technologies, and the Future of Human Intelligence.* New York, Oxford University Press.

Clark, Christopher, and Wolfram Kaiser, eds. 2003. *Culture Wars: Secular-Catholic Conflicts in Nineteenth-Century Europe.* Cambridge: Cambridge University Press.

Cohen, Morris L. 1985. *Legal Research in a Nutshell.* 4th ed. St. Paul, MN: West.

Cole, George Watson. 1935. *Postcards, the World in Miniature: A Plan for Their Systematic Arrangement.* Pasadena, CA: Privately published.

Coleman, D. 1997. *Groupware: Collaborative Strategies for Corporate LANS and Intranets.* Upper Saddle River, NJ: Prentice Hall.

Collier, Charles W. 1991. The Use and Abuse of Humanistic Theory in Law: Re-Examining the Assumptions of Interdisciplinary Legal Scholarship. *Duke Law Journal* 41:191–272.

Comte, August. 1830. *Cours de Philosophie Positive, vol. 1, Cours De Philosophie Positive, Tome Premier, Contenant les Préliminaires Généraux et la Philosophie Mathématique.* 6 vols. Paris: Bachelier.

Cranton, Patricia. 1994. *Understanding and Promoting Transformative Learning: A Guide for Educators of Adults.* San Francisco: Jossey-Bass.

Crocombe, Ronald. 1964. *Land Tenure in the Cook Islands.* Melbourne: Oxford University Press.

D'Andrade, Roy. 2002. Cultural Darwinism and Language. *American Anthropologist* 104:223–32.

Deleuze, Gilles, and Felix Guattari. 1983. *Anti-Oedipus: Capitalism and Schizophrenia.* Minneapolis: University of Minnesota Press.

———. 1987 [1980]. *A Thousand Plateaus: Capitalism and Schizophrenia.* Minneapolis: University of Minnesota Press.

Derry, Sharon J., Lori Adams DuRussel, and Angela M. O'Donnell. 1998. Individual and Distributed Cognitions in Interdisciplinary Teamwork: A Developing Case Study and Emerging Theory. *Educational Psychology Review* 10:25–56.

Dillon, Michael. 2000. Poststructuralism, Complexity, and Poetics. *Theory, Culture, and Society* 17:1–26.

DiMaggio, Paul. 2001. Introduction: Making Sense of the Contemporary Firm and Prefiguring Its Future. In *The Twenty-First-Century Firm: Changing Economic Organization in International Perspective,* ed. P. DiMaggio, 3–30. Princeton, NJ: Princeton University Press.

DiMaggio, Paul, John Evans, and Bethany Bryson. 1996. Have Americans' Social Attitudes Become More Polarized? *American Journal of Sociology* 102:690–755.

DiMarco, Anthony M. 1997. *Comparative Methods for Advocating Information Technology Investments.* Presentation at the 1997 Annual Conference of the Geospatial Information and Technology Association (GITA). http://www.Gisdevelopment.Net/Proceedings/Gita/1997/Feiafgis/Fei034.Shtml (accessed April 27, 2004).

Dolby, R. G. A. 1979. Classification of the Sciences: The Nineteenth-Century Tradition. In *Classifications in Their Social Context,* ed. R. F. Ellen and D. Reason, 167–93. London: Academic Press.

Downey, Gary Lee. 1995. Human Agency in CAD/CAM Technology. In *The Cyborg Handbook,* ed. C. H. Gray, 363–70. New York: Routledge.

Downey, Gary Lee, and Juan D. Rogers. 1995. On the Politics of Theorizing in a Postmodern Academy. *American Anthropologist* 97:269–81.

Doyle, John. 1992. Westlaw and the American Digest Classification Scheme. *Law Library Journal* 84:229–58.

Drège, Jean-Pierre. 1991. *Les Bibliothèques en Chine au Temps des Manuscrits (Jusqu'au Xe Siècle). Publications De L'Ecole Française D'Extrême-Orient, CLXI.* Paris: Ecole Française d'Extrême-Orient.

Dreyfus, Hubert. 1992. *What Computers Still Can't Do: A Critique of Artificial Reason.* Cambridge: MIT Press.

Dudbridge, Glen. 2000. *Lost Books of Medieval China: The Panizzi Lectures, 1999.* London: British Library.

Dumit, Joseph, and Robbie Davis-Floyd. 1998. Cyborg Babies: Children of the Third Millennium. In *Cyborg Babies: From Techno-Sex to Techno-Tots,* ed. R. Davis-Floyd and J. Dumit, 1–18. New York: Routledge.

Durkheim, Emile. 1933 [1893]. *The Division of Labor in Society.* New York: Macmillan.

Ellen, Roy. 1993. *The Cultural Relations of Classification: An Analysis of Nuaulu Animal Categories From Central Seram. Cambridge Studies in Social and Cultural Anthropology, 91.* Cambridge: Cambridge University Press.

Ellen, Roy F., and David Reason, eds. 1979. *Classifications in Their Social Context.* London: Academic Press.

Ess, Charles. 2001. What's Culture Got To Do With It? Cultural Collisions in the Electronic Global Village, Creative Interferences, and the Rise of Culturally-Mediated Computing. In *Culture, Technology, Communication: Towards an Intercultural Global Village,* ed. Charles Ess and Fay Sudweeks, 1–50. Albany: State University of New York Press.

Evans, John. 2003. Have Americans' Attitudes Become More Polarized?—An Update. *Social Science Quarterly* 84:71–90.

Farquhar, Carolyn R. 1998. *Middle Managers are Back: How Companies Have Come to Value Their Middle Managers Again.* Report for the Public Service Commission of the Government of Canada. http://www.Managers-Gestionnaires.Gc.Ca/Career_development/Middle_managers_are_back/Conf_e.Shtml (accessed April 30, 2004).

Fernback, Jan. 1997. The Individual within the Collective: Virtual Ideology and the Realization of Collective Principles. In *Virtual Culture: Identity and Communication in Cybersociety,* ed. S. G. Jones, 36–54. Thousand Oaks, CA: Sage.

Fish, Stanley. 1980. *Is There a Text in This Class?* Cambridge: Harvard University Press.

Flew, Anthony. 1995. *Thinking about Social Thinking.* 2d ed. Amherst, NY: Prometheus Books.

Foucault, Michel. 1970. *The Order of Things: An Archaeology of the Human Sciences.* New York: Vintage.

———. 1977. *Discipline and Punish.* New York: Pantheon.

———. 1980. *Power/Knowledge.* New York: Pantheon.

———. 1984. *The Foucault Reader.* New York: Pantheon.

Fromm, Erich. 1941. *Escape From Freedom.* New York: Rinehart & Company.

Gauch, Susan, Jason Chaffee, and Alexander Pretschner. 2002. *Ontology-Based User Profiles for Search and Browsing.*

Geertz, Clifford. 1973a. The Growth of Culture and the Evolution of Mind. In *The Interpretation of Cultures,* 55–83. New York: Basic Books.

———. 1973b. The Impact of the Concept of Culture on the Concept of Man. In *The Interpretation of Cultures,* 33–54. New York: Basic Books.

———. 1983. The Way We Think Now: Toward an Ethnography of Modern Thought. In *Local Knowledge: Further Essays in Interpretive Anthropology*, 147–63. New York: Basic Books.

———. 2000. *Available Light: Anthropological Reflections on Philosophical Topics*. Princeton, NJ: Princeton University Press.

Gellner, Ernest. 1992. *Postmodernism, Reason, and Religion*. New York: Routledge.

Gergen, Kenneth J. 1991. *The Saturated Self: Dilemmas of Identity in Contemporary Life*. New York: Basic Books.

———. 1994. Exploring the Postmodern: Perils or Potentials? *American Psychologist* 49:412–16.

Gilmore, Grant. 1977. *The Ages of American Law*. New Haven: Yale University Press.

Gilreath, James, and Douglas L. Wilson, eds. 1989. *Thomas Jefferson's Library: A Catalog with the Entries in His Own Order*. Washington, DC: Library of Congress.

Goody, Jack. 1986. *The Logic of Writing and the Organization of Society*. Cambridge: Cambridge University Press.

Goonatilake, Suran. 1995. Intelligent Systems for Finance and Business: An Overview. In *Intelligent Systems for Finance and Business*, ed. S. Goonatilake and P. Treleaven, 1–28. New York: John Wiley & Sons.

Graubard, Mark. 1953. *Astrology and Alchemy: Two Fossil Sciences*. New York: Philosophical Library.

Gray, Madison J. 2003. Man vs. Machine Series Ends 3–3. *Lawrence Journal-World*, p. A:2.

Grossberg, Lawrence. 1996. Toward a Genealogy of the State of Cultural Studies. In *Disciplinarity and Dissent in Cultural Studies*, ed. C. Nelson and D. P. Gaonkar, 131–47. New York: Routledge.

Grossman, George S. 1994. *Legal Research: Historical Foundations of the Electronic Age*. New York: Oxford University Press.

Gunkel, David. 2000. We Are Borg: Cyborgs and the Subject of Communication. *Communication Theory* 10:332–47.

Gurak, Laura J. 1997. *Persuasion and Privacy in Cyberspace*. New Haven: Yale University Press.

Hakken, David. 1999. *Cyborgs@Cyberspace? An Ethnographer Looks to the Future*. New York: Routledge.

Halvorson, T. R. 2000. *Law of the Super Searchers: The Online Secrets of Top Legal Researchers*. Medford, NJ: CyberAge Books.

Hanson, F. Allan. 1970. *Rapan Lifeways: Society and History on a Polynesian Island*. Boston: Little, Brown.

———. 1975. *Meaning in Culture*. London: Routledge & Kegan Paul.

———. 1979. Does God Have a Body? Truth, Reality, and Cultural Relativism. *Man* 14:515–29.

———. 1981. Anthropologie und die Rationalitätsdebatte. In *Der Wissenschaftler und das Irrationale*, ed. Hans Peter Duerr, vol. 1, 245–72. Frankfurt am Main: Syndikat.

———. 1983. When the Map Is the Territory: Art in Maori Culture. In *Structure and Cognition in Art*, ed. D. K. Washburn, 74–89. Cambridge: Cambridge University Press.

———. 1985. Relativism. In *The Social Science Encyclopedia*, ed. Adam and Jessica Kuper, 696–98. London: Routledge & Kegan Paul.

———. 1989. The Making of the Maori: Culture Invention and Its Logic. *American Anthropologist* 91:890–902.

———. 1995. Racism and Relativism. *Tikkun* (November–December) 10(6):63–66.

———. 1997. Empirical Anthropology, Postmodernism, and the Invention of Tradition. In *Present is Past: Some Uses of Tradition in Native Societies*, ed. Marie Mauzé, 195–214. Lanham, MD: University Press of America.

———. 2002. From Key Numbers to Keywords: How Automation Has Transformed the Law. *Law Library Journal* 94:563–600.

———. 2004a. From Classification to Indexing: How Automation Transforms the Way We Think. *Social Epistemology* 18:333–56.

———. 2004b. The New Superorganic. *Current Anthropology* 45:467–82.

———. 2005. Culture against Society. *Society* (July/August) 42(5):65–68.

Hanson, F. Allan, and Louise Hanson. 1983. *Counterpoint in Maori Culture*. London: Routledge & Kegan Paul.

Hanson, F. Allan and Rex Martin. 1973. The Problem of Other Cultures. *Philosophy of the Social Sciences* 3:191–208.

Haraway, Donna J. 1991. *Simians, Cyborgs, and Women: The Reinvention of Nature*. London: Free Association Books.

———. 1997. Mice into Wormholes: A Comment on the Nature of No Nature. In *Cyborgs & Citadels*, ed. G. L. Downey and J. Dumit, 209–43. Santa Fe, NM: School of American Research Press.

Harrington, W. G. 1984–1985. A Brief History of Computer-Assisted Legal Research. *Law Library Journal* 77:543–56.

Harris, Marvin. 1999. *Theories of Culture in Postmodern Times*. Walnut Creek, CA: Altamira.

Hasnas, John. 1995. Back to the Future: From Critical Legal Studies Forward to Legal Realism, or How Not to Miss the Point of the Indeterminacy Argument. *Duke Law Journal* 45:84–132.

Henry, Jules. 1963. *Culture against Man*. New York: Random House.

Herrnstein, Richard J., and Charles Murray. 1994. *The Bell Curve: Intelligence and Class Structure in American Life*. New York: Free Press.

Hickey, Thomas B., and Diane Vizine-Goetz. 1999. *The Role of Classification in CORC.* http://www.Oclc.Org/Research/Publications/Arr/1999/Hickey/Corc.Htm (accessed June 1, 2002).

Hieb, Louis A. 1979. Hopi World View. In *Handbook of North American Indians, Vol. 9:1,* ed. A. Ortiz, 577–80. Washington, DC: Smithsonian Institution.

Hits and Misses. 1998. *Economist* 347:93–94.

Hoeflich, M. H. 2001. *The Lawyer as Pragmatic Reader: The History of Legal Common-Placing.* Lecture manuscript.

Hoeflich, Michael H., and Jasonne Grabher O'Brien. Forthcoming. The Establishment of Normative Legal Texts: The Beginnings of the Jus Commune. In *History of Medieval Canon Law, Vol. 6: The History of Medieval Canon Law in the Classical Period, 1140–1234,* ed. Wilfried Hartmann and Kenneth Pennington. Washington, DC: Catholic University Press.

Hollmer, Mark. 2003. Northern Light Rescued from Bankruptcy. http://www.Bizjournals.Com/Boston/Stories/2003/05/19/Daily35.html (accessed August 12, 2004).

Hout, Michael. 1999. Abortion Politics in the United States, 1972–1994: From Single Issue to Iideology. *Gender Issues* 17(2):3–34.

Huarte, Juan. 1959 [1594]. *Examen de Ingenios: The Examination of Mens Wits* (1594). Gainesville, FL: Scholars' Facsimiles and Reprints.

Humphreys, K. W., ed. 1990. *The Friars' Libraries.* London: British Library.

Hunn, E. 1975a. A Measure of the Degree of Correspondence of Folk to Scientific Biological Classification. *American Ethnologist* 2:309–27.

———. 1975b. The Tenejapa Tzeltal Version of the Animal Kingdom. *Anthropological Quarterly* 48:14–30.

Hunter, James Davison. 1991. *Culture Wars: The Struggle to Define America.* New York: Basic Books.

———. 1994. *Before the Shooting Begins: Searching for Democracy in the American Culture War.* New York: Free Press.

Huntington, Samuel P. 1993. The Clash of Civilizations? *Foreign Affairs* (Summer 1993): 22–49.

Hutchins, Edwin. 1991. The Social Organization of Distributed Cognition. In *Perspectives on Socially Shared Cognition,* ed. L. B. Resnick, J. M. Livine, and S. D. Teasley, 283–307. Washington, DC: American Psychological Association.

———. 1995. *Cognition in the Wild.* Cambridge: MIT Press.

Jacso, Peter. 1999. More Search Engines: Hype and Reality. *Information Today* 16:30–31.

Jarvie, I. C. 1964. *The Revolution in Anthropology.* New York: Humanities Press.

———. 1984. *Rationality and Relativism: In Search of a Philosophy and History of Anthropology.* London: Routledge & Kegan Paul.

Jones, Richard H. 2000. *Reductionism: Analysis and the Fullness of Reality.* Lewisburg, PA: Bucknell University Press.

Jones, Steven G. 1997. The Internet and its Social Landscape. In *Virtual Culture: Identity and Communication in Cybersociety,* ed. Steven G. Jones, 7–35. Thousand Oaks, CA: Sage.

———, ed. 1995. *Cybersociety: Computer-Mediated Communication and Community.* Thousand Oaks, CA: Sage.

Jonker, Frederick. 1964. *Indexing Theory, Indexing Methods, and Search Devices.* New York: The Scarecrow Press.

Joy, Lynn S. 1991. Interpreting Nature: Gassendi versus Diderot on the Unity of Knowledge. In *The Shapes of Knowledge From the Renaissance to the Enlightenment,* ed. D. R. Kelley and R. H. Popkin, 123–34. Dordrecht: Kluwer.

Kamenka, Eugene, and Alice Erh-Soon Tay. 1975. Beyond Bourgeois Individualism: The Contemporary Crisis in Law and Legal Ideology. In *Feudalism, Capitalism, and Beyond,* ed. E. Kamenka and R. S. Neale, 126–44. London: Edward Arnold.

Kaplan, Soren. 2002. *Models for Group and Occasional Collaboration.* http://www.Icohere.Com/Collaboration_Models.Pdf (accessed April 30, 2004).

Katsh, M. Ethan. 1989. *The Electronic Media and the Transformation of Law.* New York: Oxford University Press.

———. 1993. Law in a Digital World: Computer Networks and Cyberspace. *Villanova Law Review* 38:403–85.

———. 1995. *Law in a Digital World.* New York: Oxford University Press.

Katz, Michael B. 1989. *The Undeserving Poor: From the War on Poverty to the War on Welfare.* New York: Pantheon.

Kay, Paul. 1971. Taxonomy and Semantic Contrast. *Language* 47:866–87.

Keeble, Leigh and Brian D. Loader. 2001. Community Informatics: Themes and Issues. In *Community Informatics,* ed. Leigh Keeble and Brian D. Loader, 1–10. New York: Routledge.

Kelley, Donald R., and Richard H. Popkin, eds. 1991. *The Shapes of Knowledge From the Renaissance to the Enlightenment.* Dordrecht: Kluwer.

Kesby, John D. 1979. The Rangi Classification of Animals and Plants. In *Classifications in Their Social Context,* ed. R. F. Ellen and D. Reason, 33–56. London: Academic Press.

Kincaid, Harold. 1997. *Individualism and the Unity of Science: Essays on Reduction, Explanation, and the Special Sciences.* Lanham, MD: Rowman & Littlefield.

Kissam, Philip C. 1986. The Decline of Law School Professionalism. *University of Pennsylvania Law Review* 134:251–325.

Klein, Julie Thompson. 1990. *Interdisciplinarity: History, Theory, and Practice.* Detroit: Wayne State University Press.

Koch, Traugott, Michael Day, Anna Brümmer, Debra Hiom, Marianne Peereboom, Alan Poulter, and Emma Worsfold. 1997. *Specification for Resource Description Methods Part 3. The Role of Classification Schemes in Internet Resource Description and Discovery.* http://www.Ukoln.Ac.Uk/Metadata/Desire/Classification/ (accessed March 26, 2002).

Kollock, Peter, and Marc A. Smith. 1999. Introduction: Communities in Cyberspace. In *Communities in Cyberspace*, ed. M. A. Smith and P. Kollock, 3–25. London: Routledge.

Krause, Margaret Maher. 1993. Look beyond LEXIS and WESTLAW: Other Computer Applications in the Practice of Law. *Law Library Journal* 85:575–82.

Kroeber, A. L. 1917. The Superorganic. *American Anthropologist* 19:163–213.

Kurzweil, Ray. 1999. *The Age of Spiritual Machines: When Computers Exceed Human Intelligence.* New York: Viking.

Kustron, Konnie G. 1997. Searching the World Wide Web. *Research Management Quarterly* 31:8–11.

Landow, George P. 1997 [1992]. *Hypertext 2.0: The Convergence of Contemporary Critical Theory and Technology.* 2d ed. Baltimore, MD: Johns Hopkins University Press.

Latour, Bruno. 1987. *Science in Action: How to Follow Scientists and Engineers through Society.* Cambridge: Cambridge University Press.

———. 1988. *The Pasteurization of France.* Cambridge: Harvard University Press.

Lave, Jean. 1991. Situating Learning in Communities of Practice. In *Perspectives on Socially Shared Cognition*, ed. L. B. Resnick, J. M. Livine, and S. D. Teasley, 63–82. Washington, DC: American Psychological Association.

Law, John. 1987. Technology and Heterogeneous Engineering: The Case of Portuguese Expansion. In *The Social Construction of Technological Systems: New Directions in the Sociology and History of Technology*, ed. W. E. Bijker, T. P. Hughes, and T. J. Pinch, 111–34. Cambridge: MIT Press.

———. 1991. Introduction: Monsters, Machines, and Sociotechnical Relations. In *A Sociology of Monsters: Essays of Power, Technology, and Domination*, ed. J. Law, 1–23. London: Routledge.

———. 1999. After ANT: Complexity, Naming, and Topology. In *Actor Network Theory and After*, ed. J. Law and J. Hassard, 1–14. Oxford: Blackwell.

Levi-Strauss, Claude. 1985. *The View From Afar.* New York: Basic Books.

Lewis, Bernard. 2002. *What Went Wrong? Western Impact and Middle Eastern Response.* Oxford: Oxford University Press.

Lien, Molly Warner. 1998. Technocentrism and the Soul of the Common Law Lawyer. *American University Law Review* 48:85–134.

Lifton, Robert Jay. 1979. *The Broken Connection: On Death and the Continuity of Life.* New York: Simon & Schuster.

———. 1993. *The Protean Self: Human Resilience in an Age of Fragmentation.* New York: Basic Books.

Lindholm, Charles. 1997. Logical and Moral Dilemmas of Postmodernism. *Journal of the Royal Anthropological Institute* 3:747–60.

Lopez, Alejandro, Scott Atran, John D. Coley, and Douglas L. Medin. 1997. The Tree of Life: Universal and Cultural Features of Folkbiological Taxonomies and Inductions. *Cognitive Psychology* 32:251–95.

Lovejoy, Arthur O. 1964 [1936]. *The Great Chain of Being.* Cambridge, MA: Harvard University Press.

Lynch, Michael P. 2004. *True to Life: Why Truth Matters.* Cambridge: MIT Press.

Machlup, Fritz. 1982. *The Branches of Learning. Knowledge: Its Creation, Distribution, and Economic Significance, vol. 2.* Princeton, NJ: Princeton University Press.

Machrone, Bill. 1996. The End of Common Experience. *PC Magazine,* October 22, p. 85.

Malthus, T. R. 1992 [1803]. *An Essay on the Principle of Population.* Cambridge: Cambridge University Press.

Maze, Susan, David Moxley, and Donna J. Smith. 1997. *Authoritative Guide to Web Search Engines.* New York: Neal-Schuman.

Maznevski, M. L., and K. M. Chudoba. 2000. Bridging Space over Time: Global Virtual Team Dynamics and Effectiveness. *Organization Science* 11:473–92.

McIntosh, C. 1969. *The Astrologers and Their Creed: An Historical Outline.* New York: Praeger.

McLuhan, Marshall. 1994 [1964]. *Understanding Media: The Extensions of Man.* Cambridge: MIT Press.

Merryman, John Henry. 1977. Toward a Theory of Citations: An Empirical Study of the Citation Practice of the California Supreme Court in 1950, 1960, and 1970. *Southern California Law Review* 50:381–428.

Meigs, Anna S. 1984. *Food, Sex, and Pollution: A New Guinea Religion.* New Brunswick: Rutgers University Press.

Miller, Alan S. and John P. Hoffmann. 1999. The Growing Divisiveness: Culture Wars or a War of Words? *Social Forces* 78:721–52.

Moore, Joyce L., and Thomas R. Rocklin. 1998. The Distribution of Distributed Cognition: Multiple Interpretations and Uses. *Educational Psychology Review* 10:97–113.

Moravec, Hans P. 1988. *Mind Children: The Future of Robot and Human Intelligence.* Cambridge, MA: Harvard University Press.

Morgan, Lewis Henry. 1877. *Ancient Society.* Chicago: C. H. Kerr.

Muller, Hermann J. 1959. The Guidance of Human Evolution. *Perspectives in Biology and Medicine* 3:1–43.

Munday, R. 1983. The Limits of Citation Determined. *Law Society Gazette* 80:1337–1339.

Murray, Charles. 1984. *Losing Ground: American Social Policy, 1950–1980.* New York: Basic Books.

Myers, Fred R. 1986. *Pintupi Country, Pintupi Self: Sentiment, Place, and Politics among Western Desert Aborigines*. Washington, DC: Smithsonian Institution Press.

Needham, Rodney. 1979. *Symbolic Classification*. Santa Monica, CA: Goodyear.

Neihardt, John G. 1972 [1932]. *Black Elk Speaks*. New York: Pocket Books.

Nelson, Cary, and Dilip Parameshwar Gaonkar. 1996. Cultural Studies and the Politics of Disciplinarity: An Introduction. In *Disciplinarity and Dissent in Cultural Studies*, ed. C. Nelson and D. P. Gaonkar, 1–19. New York: Routledge.

Norman, Donald A. 1997. Symbiosis: Why It's Good That Computers Don't Work Like the Brain. *Computerworld* 31:87–88.

Notess, Greg R. 1998. Northern Light: New Search Engine for the Web and Full-Text Articles. *Database* 2:32–37.

Oliver, Douglas. 1974. *Ancient Tahitian Society*. 3 vols. Honolulu: University Press of Hawaii.

Olivieri, Grazia Tonelli. 1991. Galen and Francis Bacon: Faculties of the Soul and the Classification of Knowledge. In *The Shapes of Knowledge From the Renaissance to the Enlightenment*, ed. D. R. Kelley and R. H. Popkin, 61–81. Dordrecht: Kluwer.

Ong, Walter J. 1958. *Ramus, Method, and the Decay of Dialogue: From the Art of Discourse to the Art of Reason*. Cambridge, MA: Harvard University Press.

Ostroff, Frank. 1999. *The Horizontal Organization: What the Organization of the Future Looks Like and How It Delivers Value to Customers*. New York: Oxford University Press.

Ottino, Paul. 1972. *Rangiroa: Parente, Residence Et Terres Dans Un Atol Polynesien*. Paris: Editions Cujas.

Panoff, Michel. 1964. *Les Structures Agraires on Polynesie Francaise*. Paris: Ecole Pratique des Hautes Etudes.

Park, Rev. Roswell. 1847. *Pantology, or, a Systematic Survey of Human Knowledge*. 4th ed. Philadelphia: Alexander McCay.

Posner, Richard A. 1987. The Decline of Law As an Autonomous Discipline 1962–1987. *Harvard Law Review* 100:761–81.

Poster, Mark. 1990. *The Mode of Information: Poststructuralism and Social Context*. Chicago: University of Chicago Press.

———. 1997. Cyberdemocracy: The Internet and the Public Sphere. In *Virtual Politics: Identity and Community in Cyberspace*, ed. D. Holmes, 212–28. London: Sage.

———. 2001. *What's the Matter with the Internet? Electronic Mediations*, vol. 3. Minneapolis: University of Minnesota Press.

Postman, Neil. 1992. *Technopoly: The Surrender of Culture to Technology*. New York: Knopf.

Ravindran, Devanand and Susan Gauch. 2004. Exploiting Hierarchical Relationships in Conceptual Search. Thirteenth International Conference on Information and Knowledge Management, pp. 238–39. Washington, DC: CIKM, November 2004.

Rawlins, Gregory J. E. 1997. *Slaves of the Machine: The Quickening of Computer Technology.* Cambridge: MIT Press.

Reed, Stephen L., and Douglas B. Lenat. 2002. *Mapping Ontologies into Cyc.* http://www.Cyc.Com/Doc/White_papers/Mapping-Ontologies-Into-Cyc_v31.pdf (accessed July 1, 2003).

Resnick, Lauren B., John M. Levine, and Stephanie D. Teasley, eds. 1991. *Perspectives on Socially Shared Cognition.* Washington, DC: American Psychological Association.

Rheingold, Howard. 1993. *The Virtual Community: Homesteading on the Electronic Frontier.* Reading, MA: Addison-Wesley.

Richmond, Phyllis A. 1965. *Aspects of Research in the Art and Science of Classification.* FID/CR Report Series, 3. Copenhagen: Danish Center for Documentation.

Rider, A. Fremont. 1969. The Story of D.C., 1876–1951. In *The Catalog and Cataloging,* ed. A. R. Rowland, 284–90. Hamden, CT: The Shoe String Press.

Roitblat, Herbert L. 2000. *DolphinSearch Technology White Paper: A Specialized Search Engine.* http://www.Dolphinsearch.Com/Downloads/DsWhitePaper2001.pdf (accessed July 12, 2003).

Rooney, Ellen. 1990. Discipline and Vanish: Feminism, the Resistance to Theory, and the Politics of Cultural Studies. *Differences* 2(3):14–28.

Rorty, Richard. 1982. *Consequences of Pragmatism (Essays: 1972–1980).* Minneapolis: University of Minnesota Press.

Sabel, Charles F., and Jonathan Zeitlin, eds. 1997. *World of Possibilties: Flexibility and Mass Production in Western Industrialization.* Paris: Maison des Sciences de l'Homme.

Sahlins, Marshall. 1976. Colors and Culture. *Semiotica* 16:1–22.

Said, Edward W. 1985. *Beginnings: Intention and Method.* New York: Columbia University Press.

———. 2000. *Review of Power: Essential Works of Foucault, 1954–1984,* vol. 3, by M. Foucault. *New York Times Book Review,* December 17, pp. 16–17.

Sakoian, F., and L. Acker. 1973. *The Astrologer's Handbook.* New York: Harper and Row.

Sawhill, Isabel V. 1988. Poverty in the U.S.: Why Is It So Persistent? *Journal of Economic Literature* 26:1073–1119.

Schanck, Peter C. 1990a. Taking Up Barkan's Challenge: Looking at the Judicial Process and Legal Research. *Law Library Journal* 82:1–22.

———. 1990b. The Last Word (I Hope). *Law Library Journal* 82:37.

Schauer, Frederick, and Virginia J. Wise. 1997. Legal Positivism As Legal Information. *Cornell Law Review* 82:1080–1109.

———. 2000. Nonlegal Information and the Delegalization of Law. *Journal of Legal Studies* 29:495–515.

Schwartz, Aaron. 2002 (last modified May 1, 2002). *The Semantic Web in Breadth* http://Logicerror.Com/SemanticWeb-Long#acks (accessed June 10, 2003).

Schwartz, Bernard. 1993. *Main Currents in American Legal Thought.* Durham, NC: Carolina Academic Press.

Selinger, Evan, and Timothy Engström. n.d. On Naturally Embodied Cyborgs: Identities, Metaphors, and Models. *Janus Head,* forthcoming.

Selya, Bruce M. 1994. Publish and Perish: The Fate of the Federal Appeals Judge in the Information Age. *Ohio State Law Journal* 55:405–14.

Shafer, Keith E. 1997. *Evaluating Scorpion Results.* http://www.Oclc.Org/Research/Publications/Arr/1997/Shafer/Eval_scorpion/Eval_sc.html (accessed June 2, 2002).

Shank, Gary. 1993. Abductive Multiloguing: The Semiotic Dynamics of Navigating the Net. *The Arachnet Electronic Journal on Virtual Culture,* 1. http://ibiblio.org/pub/academic/communications/papers/ejvc/SHANK.VINI (accessed June 15, 2006).

Shank, Gary, and Donald Cunningham. 1996. Mediated Phospher Dots: Toward a Post-Cartesian Model of CMC via the Semiotic Superhighway. In *Philosophical Perspectives on Computer-Mediated Communication,* ed. C. Ess, 27–41. Albany: State University of New York Press.

Shapiro, Sidney A., and Richard E. Levy. 1995. Judicial Incentives and Indeterminacy in Substantive Review of Administrative Decisions. *Duke Law Journal* 44:1051–1080.

Shweder, Richard A. 1994. *Keep Your Mind Open. Review of The Protean Self: Human Resilience in an Age of Fragmentation,* by R. J. Lifton. *New York Times Book Review,* February 20, p. 16.

———. 2002 "What about Female Genital Mutilation?" and Why Understanding Culture Matters in the First Place. In *Engaging Cultural Differences: The Multicultural Challenge in Liberal Democracies,* ed. Richard A. Shweder, Martha Minow, and Hazel Rose Markus, 216–51. New York: Russell Sage Foundation.

Slaughter, Mary M. 1982. *Universal Languages and Scientific Taxonomy in the Seventeenth Century.* Cambridge: Cambridge University Press.

Smith, Marc A. 1999. Invisible Crowds in Cyperspace: Mapping the Social Structure of the Usenet. In *Communities in Cyberspace,* ed. M. A. Smith and P. Kollock, 195–219. London: Routledge.

Smith, Marc A., and Peter Kollock, eds. 1999. *Communities in Cyberspace.* London: Routledge.

Star, Susan Leigh. 1991. Power, Technology, and the Phenomenology of Conventions: On Being Allergic to Onions. In *A Sociology of Monsters: Essays of Power, Technology, and Domination,* ed. J. Law, 26–56. London: Routledge.

Strathern, Andrew, and Pamela J. Stewart. 1998. Seeking Personhood: Anthropological Accounts of Local Concepts in Mount Hagen. *Oceania* 68:170–88.

Strout, Ruth French. 1969. The Development of the Catalog and Cataloging Codes. In *The Catalog and Cataloging,* ed. A. R. Rowland, 3–33. Hamden, CT: The Shoe String Press.

Subramanian, Srividhya, and Keith E. Shafer. 1997. *Clustering.* http://www.Oclc.Org/Research/Publications/Arr/1997/Shafer/Clustering/Clustering.htm (accessed June 1, 2002).

Suchman, Lucy. 2000. *Human/Machine Reconsidered.* http://www.Comp.Lancs.Ac.Uk/Sociology/Papers/Suchman-Human-Machine-Reconsidered.pdf (accessed August 24, 2004).

Tehranian, Majid. 1996. The End of University? *The Information Society* 12:441–47.

Tiryakian, Edward A. 1994. Revisiting Sociology's First Classic: The Division of Labor in Society and Its Actuality. *Sociological Forum* 9:3–16.

Toner, Robin. 2004. The Culture Wars, Part II. *New York Times,* February 29, 2004 sec. 4: pp. 1, 3.

Toulmin, Stephen. 1982. *The Return to Cosmology: Postmodern Science and the Theology of Nature.* Berkeley: University of California Press.

Trinca, Helen. 2004. Do I Still Need a Consultant? *AFR Boss.* http://www.afrboss.com.au/marticle.asp?doc_id=23004&rgid=2&listed_months=3 (accessed June 21, 2006).

Turkle, Sherry. 1995. *Life on the Screen: Identity in the Age of the Internet.* New York: Simon & Schuster.

———. 1998. Cyborg Babies and Cy-Dough-Plasm: Ideas about Self and Life in the Culture of Simulation. In *Cyborg Babies: From Techno-Sex to Techno-Tots,* ed. R. Davis-Floyd and J. Dumit, 317–29. New York: Routledge.

Turner, Terrence. 1993. Anthropology and Multiculturalism: What Is Anthropology That Multiculturalists Should Be Mindful of It? *Cultural Anthropology* 8:411–29.

Udargo, Max. 2004. *Cheney's Colorful Comment.* http://www.Democraticunderground.Com/Articles/04/06/P/30_colorful.html (accessed March 25, 2005).

Usher, Robin, Ian Bryant, and Rennie Johnston. 1997. *Adult Education and the Postmodern Challenge: Learning beyond the Limits.* London: Routledge.

Veith, Ilza, trans. 1966 [1949]. *The Yellow Emperor's Classic of Internal Medicine.* Berkeley: University of California Press.

Vreeland, Robert C., and Bert J. Dempsey. 1996. Toward a Truly Seamless Web: Bringing Order to Law on the Internet. *Law Library Journal* 88:469–87.

Wagner, Roy. 1991. The Fractal Person. In *Big Men and Great Men: Personification of Power in Melanesia,* ed. M. Godelier and M. Strathern, 159–73. Cambridge: Cambridge University Press.

Walzer, Michael. 1994. *Thick and Thin: Moral Argument at Home and Abroad.* Notre Dame, IN: University of Notre Dame Press.

Ward, Joyce. 1999. *Indexing and Classification at Northern Light. Powerpoint Presentation to CENDI Conference on "Controlled Vocabulary and the Internet."* http://www.Dtic.Mil/Cendi/Pres_arc.html (accessed June 2, 2002).

Washburn, Sherwood L. 1959. Speculations on the Interrelations of Tools and Biological Evolution. In *The Evolution of Man's Capacity for Culture*, ed. J. M. Spuhler, 21–31. Detroit, MI: Wayne State University Press.

Watson, Nessim. 1997. Why We Argue about Vitural Community: A Case Study of the Phish.Net Fan Community. In *Virtual Culture: Identity and Communication in Cybersociety*, ed. S. G. Jones, 102–32. Thousand Oaks, CA: Sage.

Wellman, Barry. 2001. Physical Place and Cyberplace: The Rise of Networked Individualism. In *Community Informatics*, ed. L. Keeble and B. D. Loader, 17–42. New York: Routledge.

Wellman, Barry, and Milena Gulia. 1999. Virutal Communities As Communities: Net Surfers Don't Ride Alone. In *Communities in Cyberspace*, ed. M. A. Smith and P. Kollock, 167–94. London: Routledge.

White, Leslie. 1949. *The Science of Culture*. New York: Farrar, Straus, and Giroux.

Wiggins, Richard. 2002. Of Quivers and Dolphins: New Content Handlers. *Searcher* 10:61–65.

Willson, Michele. 1997. Community in the Abstract: A Political and Ethical Dilemma? In *Virtual Politics: Identity and Community in Cyberspace*, ed. D. Holmes, 145–62. London: Sage.

Windschuttle, Keith. 2002. The Ethnocentrism of Clifford Geertz. *The New Criterion* (October): 21(2).

Wood, Martin. 1998. Agency and Organization: Toward a Cyborg Consciousness. *Human Relations* 51:1209–1226.

Woodward, Augustus B. 1816. *A System of Universal Science*. Philadelphia: Edward Earle, Harrison Hall, and Moses Thomas.

Yates, Francis A. 1966. *The Art of Memory*. Chicago: University of Chicago Press.

Zerzan, John. 1994. The Catastrophe of Postmodernism. In *Future, Primitive, and Other Essays*. Brooklyn, NY: Autonomedia.

Index